Fun with Frosting

Fun with Frosting

A Beginner's Guide to Decorating Creative, Fondant-Free Cakes

K. Callard

Skyhorse Publishing

Skyhorse Publishing books may be purchased in bulk at special discounts for sales promotion, corporate gifts, fund-raising, or educational purposes. Special editions can also be created to specifications. For details, contact the Special Sales Department, Skyhorse Publishing, 307 West 36th Street, 11th Floor, New York, NY 10018or info@skyhorsepublishing.com.

Skyhorse® and Skyhorse Publishing® are registered trademarks of Skyhorse Publishing, Inc.®, a Delaware corporation.

Visit our website at www.skyhorsepublishing.com.

10 9 8 7 6 5 4 3 2 1

Library of Congress Cataloging-in-Publication Data is available on file.

Cover design by Jane Sheppard
Cover photo credit K. Callard

Print ISBN: 978-1-5107-0763-4
Ebook ISBN: 978-1-5107-0767-2

Printed in China

AUTHOR'S NOTE

My cake decorating teacher's motto was: "Who cares what it tastes like, so long as it looks good."

Well, I care.

Cakes are made to be eaten, not just to look pretty in photos. That's why I've done my best to always put flavor first in my designs. I use candy instead of fondant, stay away from salty crackers as decorations, and try to keep the frosting levels within reason—because what's the point of having a cake if you can't eat it, too?

—K. Callard

CONTENTS

BRILLIANT BASICS

BAKING

In my opinion, nothing tastes quite as good as a homemade, from-scratch cake. But, if you're low on time/energy, or baking just isn't your thing, there's nothing wrong with making a cake from a mix. All the tools and techniques on the following pages can be used for from-scratch cakes or those made from mixes to help make your cakes turn out great.

One note of caution, though. Most cake mixes do not produce a sturdy enough cake to cut for the Creative Cutout designs in this book. I highly recommend using either the pound cake recipe in this book, or doctoring a cake mix recipe using the Cake Mix Fix instructions on page 43, to get a sturdy cake to carve.

Tools

- Stand mixer/electric mixer/hand whisk—unlike muffins, cake batter should be smooth and lump-free. I typically use my hand whisk on my Chocolate Cake (see recipe on page 42), while my Pound Cake (recipe found on page 41) needs the more thorough mixing provided by a stand or electric mixer.
- Pans—the designs in this book rely on a variety of pans that can be found in most households, or you can use disposable foil pans available at grocery stores.
- Shortening/butter/margarine/"quick release" spray—to grease your pan. I typically use shortening.
- Flour/cocoa—goes on top of the grease. I usually use cocoa for my chocolate cakes and flour for the rest.
- Pastry/basting brush—to spread the flour.
- Skewer (metal or wood is fine) or toothpick (depending on the height of your cake)—to check if the cake is done.
- Cooling racks (and a way to raise them up)—standard cooling racks only lift your cake a few inches off the counter. To increase air flow, and reduce cooling time, sit your rack on something 4–5 inches tall (I use 3–4 bean cans). Just make sure your rack is level and stable.

Techniques

Sadly, while cake decorating is an art, baking is most definitely a science. To make sure your cakes turn out well, be sure to follow all the instructions given.

Greasing the Pan

This helps keep the cake from sticking to the pan. Use about a tablespoon or so of shortening/butter/ margarine and rub it liberally around the pan, making sure to hit all the corners. Remember, cake batter expands as it cooks, so you want to bring it as far up the sides of the pan as you can.

If you're a hands-on kind of person, you can rub the shortening around with your fingers, but if you're like me and dislike greasy hands, simply put the grease on a small piece of waxed or parchment paper.

Once the pan is completely covered, add about a tablespoon of flour to the pan (or cocoa for a chocolate cake) and spread it with a pastry brush.

Knock any excess flour/cocoa off into the trash.

Measuring Ingredients

Part of following the instructions is making sure to measure accurately. Never measure ingredients over your mixing bowl—spills will land in the bowl, leaving you with too much of your ingredient.

Dry ingredients, except for brown sugar, should be scooped loosely into a dry measuring cup. Use the back of a knife to tip off any excess.

Brown sugar should be packed tightly into a dry measuring cup, as if you're making a sand castle.

Wet ingredients should be measured in a liquid measuring cup, sitting on a level surface. For best results, crouch down to look at the amount straight on.

Mixing the Ingredients

The exact requirements for each recipe will differ, but generally speaking, cake ingredients (especially eggs and butter) work best at room temperature. To speed up the process, cut your butter into small cubes and lay them out on a plate—the increased surface area makes it warm faster. In a pinch, I've also sat my butter on my preheating oven—just keep an eye on it: melted butter works differently in a recipe than softened butter.

Eggs should be cracked into a small bowl before adding to the mix—it's easier to see (and remove) little bits of shell from a small bowl than the large bowl full of batter. Also remember that raw eggs can carry bacteria—you shouldn't taste your cake until it's been fully cooked.

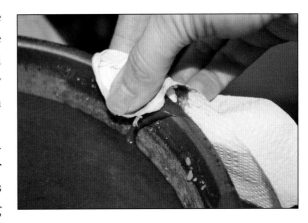

Mix your batter thoroughly until no lumps remain. Make sure to scrape the sides of the bowl with a rubber spatula as you mix to incorporate all the dry ingredients into the batter. If you notice dry patches when pouring it into the pan, you'll have to pop it back in the bowl and re-mix or else you could end up with dry bites of pure flour in your finished cake.

Pour the batter into the pan, scraping the bowl with a spatula. Wipe off any spills from the edge of the pan to prevent burnt-on bits.

How to Tell When It's Cooked

Let's face it, not all ovens are created equal. And nothing is worse than flipping your cake out of the pan and having it explode in a mushy, undercooked mess. For this reason, knowing how to tell if your cake is cooked is a must.

I tend to start checking my cakes about five minutes before the earliest end of the cooking time, and add more time from then.

Sometimes it's obvious—if you pull out your cake and it jiggles like a waterbed, it's not done.

If the skewer comes out goopy, add more time.

If the skewer comes out clean, or with just a few dry crumbs attached, you're good to go.

But other times it's harder to tell. A simple fingertip test (be careful you don't burn yourself) can give you a clue—if the cake is spongy to the touch, it's done. Remember, though: cakes cook from the outside in, so your edges may be done while your center is still liquid.

In my mind, the most reliable way to check if your cake is done is by inserting a skewer or toothpick in the center of the cake.

De-Panning

Once you pull the cake from the oven, the next step is to cool it. Place the cake *still in the pan* on your raised cooling rack and allow it to sit for ten minutes. This will give the cake enough time to

After ten minutes, run a spatula or knife around the edge of the cake to loosen it. *Be careful: the cake and pan will still be hot!* (I used to use rubber spatulas, but I found the heat from the cake was melting them. Now I use my metal off-set spatula. I just have to be careful not to scratch my pan.)

Next, sit your cake pan on something heatproof, and flip the cooling rack over on top of the cake pan (the cooling rack is now upside down).

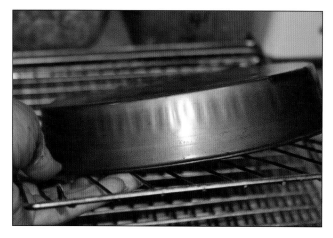

Then, flip the pan and rack over together (the rack is now right-side up, and the pan is upside down).

Gently tap the bottom of the pan. With any luck, the cake will gently slide out of the pan, onto the cooling rack. Remove the pan.

solidify (you will see it shrink away from the edges of the pan), but not enough time to cement itself to the pan.

If your cake does not come out, don't despair. Flip the cake pan back right-side up, and try to loosen it some more with a spatula. Rubber spatulas (or very thin, flexible metal ones) can bend and reach down to the bottom of the pan, helping to loosen the cake (just remember, rubber spatulas may melt from the heat).

Repeat the cooling rack flipping process above. Hopefully your cake is now on the cooling rack. If not, repeat the above instructions until your cake comes out.

If part of your cake stays in the pan, all is not lost. Warm cake is very pliable. Just remove the piece from the pan and pat it gently into place. Often, the cooling process will be enough to re-attach it to the cake. If not, frosting makes excellent glue.

Cooling

If your cake is relatively flat, leave it upside down on the rack to cool. If your cake top has puffed up, flip it back right-side up to finish cooling so it doesn't break.

Cool your cake for at least 2 hours, or until it is completely cool to the touch, before leveling, filling, and frosting.

FILLING AND ASSEMBLING

Okay, you have your two cakes (whatever size and shape you're using) cooled, but before you can start decorating, you need to fill and assemble them. This isn't a very tricky step, but make sure you leave yourself time to do it properly—you wouldn't want your pretty cake to topple!

Tools
- Cake leveler or a long, sharp serrated knife + toothpicks
- Large flat plate/cookie sheet without edges/back of a cookie sheet (depending on size of your cake)*
- Piping bag and large round tip (#12) or large star tip (#21)
- About ½ cup of the same frosting being used on the outside of the cake
- Filling (see section following, or use some of your frosting)

Used if torting your cake

Techniques
Once again, whether you've baked from scratch, or are using a mix, the following techniques will help you stack and fill your cake with ease.

How to Level a Cake
Hardly any cakes (even those baked with the magic strips) come out of the oven flat enough to stack as layers. Which means, unless you want your cake to look like the Leaning Tower of Pisa, you have to level your layers.

You have two options for tools to level the cake:

1. Cake leveler—essentially a movable piece of wire strung between two metal legs. Simply set the wire at the lowest height of the top of your cake. (Always double-check that your wire is straight.) Use a gentle sawing motion to break through the outside crust, and then apply even, gentle pressure to continue cutting the top layer off the cake. The downside? If your cake is too tall, the legs won't touch the ground, and you don't have help making sure you stay level. I have one of these, but more often than not I end up using method #2.
2. A long serrated knife

Use a gentle sawing motion to slice off the uneven top of the cake. Not sure you can level a cake by eye? Measure your desired height at various points around the outside of the cake and mark it with toothpicks.

Then, all you have to do is keep your knife straight while cutting from toothpick to toothpick, and you'll end up with an even cut.

Once your layers are flat, use your spatula to daub a bit of frosting on the bottom of your cake plate. This will act as glue to hold your cake in place.

Place one cake upside down (cut-side down) on the cake plate, pressing gently to help it stick to the frosting.

How to Torte a Cake

If you want to torte your cake (cut the layers in half to add extra filling—a great way to make a smaller cake go farther, or just make your cake look cool), do so after you have leveled it. Use the same technique as above, only this time measure half the height of the cake.

Once you've cut the cake in half, insert two toothpicks directly over each other on either side of the cut (you'll use these later).

Next, slide your flat plate or edgeless cookie sheet between the two layers—depending on the size and strength of the cake, you may need a spatula to help lift the cake onto the plate/cookie sheet.

If you don't have a flat plate or edgeless cookie sheet, you can use the back of a cookie sheet with raised edges, but you need to carefully lift the cake up and sit it on the cookie sheet (trust me and use the back of the sheet; it'll come in handy later).

Creating a Dam

Attach your large round (#12) or large star (#21) piping tip to your piping bag (see instructions on page 19). Fill the bag with the same icing you are using for the outside of the cake.

On the top of your cake layer, pipe around the outside edge of the cake, making sure to stay on top of the layer. This will create a dam to hold in the filling and help seal the edges of the layers together.

Filling Fun

This is where you can really get creative with your cake flavors. I've included recipes for three of my favorite fillings (Chocolate Ganache, Gooey Marshmallow, and Raspberry), which you can use in various combinations with the cake recipes to come up with great flavors—Double-Chocolate, Chocolate-Marshmallow S'mores, Vanilla-Raspberry, Lemon-Raspberry . . . the combinations are up to you.

Don't feel like the extra work of making a filling? Simply use some of your frosting (the same color that you're using on the outside of the cake looks best). Or open up a jar of premade pie filling, or even a cup of pudding.

Whatever your filling of choice, gently pour it onto the middle of your layer and use your spatula to spread it around, careful to keep it inside the frosting dam you piped earlier.

Be generous—it's disappointing to cut open a beautiful layer cake and not be able to see the filling between the layers. Your filling should be just a bit shorter than the height of the dam (the weight of the cake will compress it a bit, and you don't want it to overflow and escape).

Re-Assembling the Cake

Whether you've torted your cake, or are just stacking two layers, the next step is put the cake together. The most important rule to remember is that for most cakes *the bottom of the cake (the part that was in the pan) will be the top of your frosted cake!* This will help reduce crumbs and save you a lot of hassle and time when it comes to frosting.

For leveled layers, this means you will flip your second cake upside down and place the cut-edge of the top cake onto the filling.

If you torted your layer, bring your flat plate/ cookie sheet holding the top layer of cake over to the filled layer. Line up the two toothpicks you inserted, and gently shift the top layer back onto the cake filling.

Repeat the filling and assembling patterns, remembering that the top of the final layer should be the bottom of the cake (the side that was cooked in the pan).

Cupcakes

Cupcakes may be back on their way out of fashion, but to my mind, miniature cakes that you don't need a fork or plate to eat will never go out of style.

I like my cupcakes on the smaller side, sitting flush to the top of the wrapper, as opposed to puffing up and over like a muffin, so the recipes and designs here reflect that. If you're looking for more cake, check out the Cupcake-Cakeball Combo designs, which have an added cakeball on top.

The easiest, cleanest way to bake cupcakes is to use a wrapper to line the pan. If you're worried about the environment, you can buy reusable silicone liners, but they're a bit pricey, and I prefer the plain old paper ones so I can customize them to the cupcake design.

If you're using disposable liners, remember that the oil in your cupcakes will make the plain paper ones turn see-through—which is great for some of the colored cupcake designs, or even a plain white cake, but they can look dingy on a chocolate cupcake. It's pretty disheartening to pick out themed cupcake liners only to pull them out of the pan and find they're a solid chocolate brown.

The solution? Foil liners stay true, even through baking. Shiny silver and gold not your thing? Many companies now make patterned, foil-lined liners that retain their color after baking—in fact, I've even found these in the dollar store!

To make uniform-size cupcakes, I recommend finding a ladle or large spoon that holds the right amount—I use my ¼ cup dry measuring cup—and fill the cupcake liners about ⅔ of the way. Like with a whole cake, make sure you wipe any drips off the pan to prevent burnt-on crusts.

Bake your cupcakes according to instructions, and use the skewer/toothpick method outlined in the How to Tell When It's Cooked section of this book to make sure they are fully baked.

Let the cupcakes cool on a raised cooling rack for 5 to 10 minutes before removing from the pan. I use a fork or spatula to help me get them out. Careful, they'll still be quite hot!

Cool completely before filling and/or frosting.

If you want to fill your cupcakes, you have two main choices:

1. A piping bag with the cupcake-filling tip (#230). Simply fill your piping bag with your filling, stick the tip into the middle of the cupcake, and inject the filling inside.

   I've used this a few times, but I find with denser cakes (like the ones I prefer to make and have provided recipes for) not enough filling makes it into the cake.

2. Using a serrated knife to make a well in the cupcake. This is my preferred method because you can actually see how much filling is going into the cupcakes.

Using a serrated knife, cut an upside-down cone out of the center of the cupcake, being careful not to go all the way through to the bottom.

Spoon about one teaspoon of filling (depending on how large your cavity is) into the hole.

Now for the finicky part. Cut about a ¼ inch off the top (the widest end) of the cone—this will be your lid.

Sit the lid on the cupcake, on top of the filling. If you're planning on piping frosting and/or adding a cakeball, you don't have to be too precise, but if you're using one of the flat-iced designs, like the Superhero Cupcakes (page 93) or Stunning Snowflakes (page 101), then you'll need to make sure the tops end up perfectly flat.

Cakeballs

These bite-sized cake treats are among my favorite things to bake. But even better is the way they look perched on a small cupcake—so many design possibilities!

There are three ways to make cakeballs (plus a bonus no-bake way):

1. Cake pop maker—a bit like a waffle maker, this little machine plugs into the wall and cooks 12 cakeballs at a time. Simply spoon your batter into the little divots, close, and five minutes later you have a dozen cakeballs. (This is my preferred method.) Note: although

the machine's instructions say to grease the pan, I actually find they pop out better ungreased.

2. Cakeball baking pan—this one is like a cupcake pan, with a lid. Grease and flour the pan according to the instructions, spoon your batter into the semi-spheres, attach the lid, and cook in the oven according to the directions.

3. Make them out of spare cupcakes and frosting. (I promised this book wouldn't require specialty pans, so I'm including these instructions, but to be honest, I love cakeballs so much, my cakeball maker has become a necessity.)

    Simply crumble up 2 to 3 spare cupcakes into a bowl with your fingers. Add 2 to 3 tablespoons of frosting and mix together. Roll into balls and freeze.

    This method may well be one of the easiest, but it's also the sweetest. The high frosting-to-cake ratio (which is then dipped in chocolate/covered in more frosting) leaves me with a serious sugar high (and that's before I put it on top of a cupcake).

4. Use premade, plain donut holes. 'Nuff said.

    I usually work with frozen cakeballs, especially if I'm covering them with candy wafers or melted chocolate.

Covering Cakeballs

My favorite (for ease of use and taste) is covering the cakeballs with melted candy wafers. Simply heat about ¾ cup melting wafers per 4 cakeballs in a double boiler (or by microwaving them 10 seconds at a time in a microwave-safe small, deep bowl). Stir in about ¼ teaspoon of shortening to thin out the mixture (too much will make candy coating brittle), and dip cakeballs using a fork or spoon, tapping excess candy off on the side of the bowl. Leave on parchment paper to harden.

Note: If your candy wafers aren't melting—or they skip melting and go straight to burning—it means they're old. Throw them out and go buy some new ones.

Cakeballs can also be flat-iced, although it's hard to get a perfect coating (melting wafers give a much cleaner look), or piped onto (as shown in the Millions of Monsters design on page 131).

You can even dip them in melted canned frosting—but honestly, I don't find this as tasty or pretty as any of the other methods I've already mentioned.

FROSTING

There is a lot of confusion around the terms *icing* and *frosting*—some people (like me) use the terms interchangeably; others say icing is a thinner, water-sugar confection, while frosting has a butter base; and still others claim icing is the more professional term, while frosting is more . . . shall we say, rustic.

For the sake of this book, I will be using the term *frosting* because: 1) this book is aimed at home decorators and 2) I'll be working with a butter-based product for most designs.

Tools

- Stand mixer/electric mixer/hand whisk (if you're up to it)—the key to a good frosting is its smoothness, and in my opinion, an electric mixer is the way to go.
- Measuring cups and spoons—as I mentioned in the baking section, baking is science: precise measurements are a must here.
- Mixing bowl
- Containers with snap-tight lids, or bowls and cling wrap—frosting needs to be stored in airtight containers to keep it from drying out. You'll want a separate bowl for each color of frosting you're working with.
- Food dye—this can be gel or liquid. The gels give richer colors without affecting the consistency of the frosting, while the liquids are, well, liquid, and the more you add, the thinner your frosting will become. A few of the designs in this book specifically require either a gel or liquid color to work, but for the most part it's up to you which you use. More information on dyes can be found in the Creating Colors section of this chapter.
- Metal spatulas—my all-time favorite spatula is my small offset metal spatula (see photo below), which I use for just about everything. Larger offset spatulas are great for crumb-coating and flat-icing large flat areas of cake. Don't have a metal spatula? Use a rubber one (although they're better for scraping bowls) or even a blunt knife.
- Rubber spatula—for scraping the bowl
- Paper towel/napkin/dish cloth—used to wipe off your icing-coated spatula between coats. If using a non-disposable cloth, make sure it's clean to start, and rinse well with hot water after to prevent the frosting from hardening into a crusty mess.

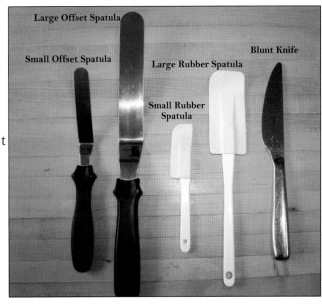

Large Offset Spatula

Small Offset Spatula

Small Rubber Spatula

Large Rubber Spatula

Blunt Knife

Techniques

Making frosting is pretty simple, but not without its pitfalls. I've outlined basic techniques here for making, coloring, and checking the consistency of homemade frosting.

Don't feel like all the hassle? You can use canned frosting to flat-ice cakes, and Decorator's Icing tubes (available at most grocery stores) to pipe designs—just be warned, the tubes of Decorator's Icing are definitely a thick consistency: perfect if you want to pipe roses, but frustrating and hard to squeeze if all you want to do is write.

Making the Frosting

First things first: you want to start with your ingredients at room temperature—that means remembering to take your butter or margarine out of the fridge early! (I almost always slow myself down by forgetting this step.) If your butter is too hard, it won't blend properly into the frosting and you'll end up with little hard chunks that don't take the dye, clog up your piping tips, and taste like straight butter.

You can tell the frosting has broken by its white, stringy appearance.

Start by mixing the wet ingredients first—your shortening and/or butter/margarine (whatever combination you're using), water, and flavoring. Remember, if your flavoring is colored, it may affect the color of your frosting. Clear vanilla extract is available at most stores that have a cake decorating section.

Mix in your confectioner's/powdered/icing sugar on medium speed, along with a dash of salt (to cut down on sweetness). Try to keep your blending time under two minutes (including blending in colors)—overmixed frosting can "break," separating the fats from the liquid.

Sadly, broken frosting tastes even worse than it looks, and once it's broken, you can't fix it; the only solution is to throw it out and start over from scratch.

Checking Consistency

There are three basic frosting consistencies:

1. *Thin Frosting* is used to crumb-coat and flat-ice cakes, as well as for piping writing and thin lines, vines, hair, and grass. Your spatula should move easily through the frosting, spreading it like soft butter. If you find your frosting isn't sticking, or that it's peeling away from the cake, it's probably too thick. Try blending in a few drops of water to thin it out.

2. *Stiff Frosting* is used for piping roses and other flowers. You should be able to scoop it up and hold it on your spatula, like full-fat cream cheese. If your frosting won't hold its shape, it's too thin. Try blending in a teaspoon or two of icing sugar to thicken it up.

3. *Medium Frosting* is used for stars and borders. Consider it the Goldilocks consistency—not too thin, not too thick, but just right. If you find your stars and borders are spreading, and not holding their shapes, your frosting is too thin: add a bit of icing sugar. If you're having trouble pushing it through the piping tip, it's too stiff: add some water.

There are lots of things that can affect the consistency of your frosting—heat, humidity, and altitude are just a few I can think of offhand. If you follow the recipe, but end up with frosting that's too thick or too thin, don't despair, just follow the directions below.

Butter, Shortening, or Margarine—Which Is the Best Fat?

Personally I prefer the taste of a half-butter, half-shortening frosting—the butter gives it a creamy flavor that's missing from shortening alone. But there are downsides. Shortening is white and produces a clearer color when dyed, while the yellow tinge of butter (and margarine) can sometimes mess up the color of your frosting. Frostings made with butter or margarine should be kept refrigerated (be sure to bring them up to room temperature before trying to frost or pipe with them).

For an easier-to-color (or pristine white), longer-lasting, refrigerator-free (although, slightly less tasty) frosting, use all shortening instead of the half-and-half combination listed in the Basic Buttercream recipe (found on page 46).

As for margarine versus butter—well, that one's up to your personal preference. Hard margarine and butter function basically the same way in the recipes, while soft margarine blends better but doesn't hold its shape as well. I recommend against using reduced-fat margarines, though, since they tend to be whipped with water and can affect the consistency of the frosting.

Fixing Consistency Problems

Consistency is one of the easiest problems to fix. A few drops of water or a teaspoon of icing sugar is typically all it takes to thin out or thicken up your frosting. I suggest using very small amounts of water or sugar, though, otherwise you'll get stuck in a loop—add too much water, too thin; add too much sugar, too thick again—until you end up diluting your flavoring and possibly breaking your frosting by overmixing it.

Creating Colors

Colors are an essential part of decorating a cake. Whether you're trying to duplicate a specific color, or making it up as you go along, knowing how to mix colors will make your cakes really pop.

Three types of food coloring exist: liquid, gel, and powder. I'll be honest, I've never used the powder form (although I have some in my kit) because I'm more comfortable using liquids or gels.

The gel colors typically work the best for tinting frosting. They have a higher pigment load, making their colors stronger, and the gel consistency doesn't water down the frosting the way the liquids can.

You can buy sets of gel coloring at most bulk and baking stores, or you can buy them individually. I tend to like mixing my own colors, so I typically work with just six gel colors: the four that come as a starter pack (red, blue, lemon yellow, and green) plus moss green (better for grass), and black.

For the most part, everything you need to know about mixing frosting colors, you learned in elementary school art class.

Red + Yellow = Orange
Red + Blue = Purple
Blue + Yellow = Green

Varying the amount of one of the colors in your mixture will get you a different tone of that color along the spectrum (e.g., Blue + just a tiny bit of Yellow = Turquoise).

If you're not used to mixing colors, I suggest you start with a small amount of dye—it's much easier to darken your colors than lighten them. Also, take note that red dye darkens as it oxidizes (mixes with air), so always let it sit a bit before using, otherwise your perfect blue-violet may become a pinky-purple by the time you serve your cake.

And speaking of darker colors, remember your frosting is starting out white, so everything starts out light. It takes a ton of red dye to make your icing red instead of pink (or black instead of gray)—which is why very few designs in this book call for red or black frosting. The dyes for those colors aren't very tasty (even the no-taste ones), and using a large amount of them can flavor your frosting.

If you want just a small amount of red or black icing (say, for mouths or eyes), I suggest buying a premade tube of Decorator's Icing from the grocery store.

If you need more than a tube, or you really can't bring yourself to buy premade frosting, then try adding about half a teaspoon of cocoa into the mix for red, or a tablespoon or so for black. The cocoa helps darken the color and has the added benefit of tasting like chocolate.

I also use cocoa powder for my brown frosting, rather than dye, because, well, chocolate goes with just about everything.

Oh, and as for gray, I find mixing green and red in with some black creates the richest color. Once again, remember your red will darken, so let it sit to make sure you don't end up with a pinky-gray. If the color does look too red, add a bit of green and vice-versa.

Crumb-Coating

Crumbs. Those pesky little guys can get in there and ruin everything when it comes to cake decorating.

Crumb-coating is creating a thin layer of frosting to seal in the crumbs, so they don't jump in and mess up your final design later.

The first trick I like to use is sweeping the cake gently with a pastry brush to knock off any stray crumbs.

Get a tablespoon or so of frosting on your spatula and hold it parallel to the side of the cake. Gently spread the frosting around—if you're frosting a round cake, sitting the cake on a turntable (lazy Susan) and rotating the cake as you spread makes the job easier.

Remember, you're just trying to create a thin layer to seal the crumbs in. Try to keep your spatula from directly touching the cake. If you get any crumbs in the frosting on your spatula, use your cloth or paper towel to wipe it clean.

Discard any frosting that has crumbs in it.

Once you've done that, generously heap on a few globs of frosting around the top of the cake. Using your spatula, lightly spread the frosting around to cover the top of the cake and over the edges.

Once all exposed areas of cake are covered with frosting, your crumb coat is done!

If you are frosting cut edges of cake (as required in the Creative Cutouts section of this book) use a flat piping tip to cover the cut edge with frosting, then gently spread it with your spatula to minimize crumb exposure.

Flat-Icing

Or should that be "Flat-Frosting"?

Flat-icing refers to spreading a thick layer of frosting over the crumb coat of the cake with your spatula.

Flat-icing is difficult to perfect—even with all my years of practice, I still can't get my cakes as perfectly smooth as some I've seen in bakeries. But don't despair. Not many of the designs in this book require flat-icing, and those that do involve decorations on top to help hide imperfections.

Here are the few tips I do have for smooth frosting:

1. Try to move your spatula in one fluid motion—the more you stop and start, the more lines you'll create.
2. Refrigerate your flat-iced cake for about 10 minutes. This should cause the frosting to form a crust. Gently touch the frosting with a finger—*If the frosting sticks to your finger, it is not dry*

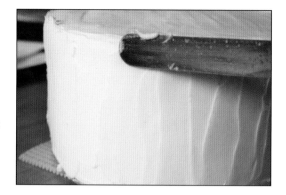

enough. Put it back in the fridge until you can touch it without it sticking to you. Lay a piece of parchment paper on top of the cake and gently smooth the frosting with your hand. Carefully peel off the paper. Repeat until the frosting is flat.

3. For the sides of layer cakes, rather than trying to get your frosting completely smooth, create a pattern instead: the easiest way is using your spatula to stripe the sides. Pick a starting point. Place your spatula flush to the cake along the bottom, and move gently upward until you reach the top of the cake. Move over ½ inch and repeat. Continue repeating around the cake until the sides of the entire cake are striped.

4. Hide imperfections with decorations.

5. Smile and pretend it was supposed to be that way. Your guests will just be happy to get cake.

Cupcakes generally do not need to be crumb-coated before flat-icing. Hold your cupcake in your non-dominant hand (I'm right-handed, so I hold it in my left hand). Daub about a tablespoon of frosting onto the cupcake with your spatula, and spread it around in a circular motion, turning the cupcake the opposite way with your other hand (you may need to re-adjust your grip partway through).

For a super-smooth coating, dip your spatula in hot-to-boiling water and smooth over the top of the cupcake using the same motion.

Storage

Storing cakes can be tricky. A flat-iced, un-cut cake will stay fresh for up to five days because the frosting holds in the moisture—that means you can bake and flat-ice your cake on Tuesday, decorate it on Wednesday, and serve it on Saturday.

However, long-term storage can affect the look of your cake. I've actually found the airtight cake carriers are the worst for making my frosting colors bleed all over each other, as they seal too tightly, so the frosting absorbs moisture from the cake.

My best tip if you're using a cake carrier is not to clamp it shut until/unless you need to carry it somewhere. I've found that by just sitting the lid on, enough air still circulates to keep my cakes looking their best.

PIPING

Now for the fun stuff. Piping is used in many of the designs in this book. Whether you just want to add style to your cupcakes, or create crazy custom creations, you need to know how to pipe.

Tools

- Piping bag—you can get reusable bags, disposable (plastic) bags, or just use a heavy-duty freezer bag with the corner snipped off.
- Piping tip(s)—whichever ones your design requires
- Piping bag coupler—this joins the tip to the piping bag. You can use tips without the coupler, but if you need to change your tip (either to use the same tip for different frostings, or different tips for the same frosting), a coupler makes things easier and cleaner.
- Spatula (whatever you've been using for flat-icing your cake)

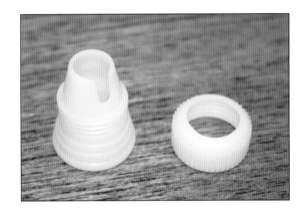

Techniques

These techniques are designed to give you the basics for sizing, filling, and holding your piping bags, plus how to clean them when you're finished.

Choosing Your Tips

For all of the designs in this book, I have listed both the description of the required tip as well as its number (e.g., medium round tip, #5)—these numbers are printed on the side of the tips. Some of the designs give you a choice of frosting tips—choose the one you think works best for you.

In a pinch, you can snip the corner off a sandwich or freezer bag and use it without a tip to pipe lines, vines, writing, and dots (replacing tips #1, 2, 3, 5, and 12, depending on how large you cut the hole).

If you're using a tube of Decorator's Icing, you need to check which tips it takes. Some tubes require special plastic tips that screw onto the tube (available where you buy Decorator's Icing), while others are compatible with your metal piping bag tips and rings.

Sizing Your Piping Bags

New piping bags (both reusable and disposable) usually come with a smaller hole than needed. If you are not using a coupler, this may be just the right size.

The hole in this piping bag is too small—there is too much space between the sides of the tip and the bag.

The hole in this piping bag is the right size—with about ⅔ of the tip out of the bag.

Slide your tip into the hole (point down)—you want it to be secure without leaving too much room around the base of the tip (otherwise frosting may try to find another way out).

If your tip is sitting securely about ⅔ of the way out of the bag, you're ready to fill.

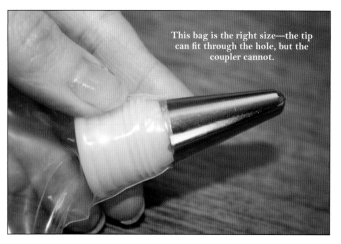

This bag is the right size—the tip can fit through the hole, but the coupler cannot.

If you're using a coupler, you need the hole to be large enough to slide the tip out when it's time to change tips. Sit your tip on the coupler (be sure to remove the ring), and slide it into the hole. If the tip slides through, but the coupler stays, your hole is the right size—attach your ring and fill your bag.

If, however, your tip doesn't fit through the hole, use your fingernail or a pencil to mark where the base of the tip is sitting. (I suggest you mark closer to the end of the bag than you think you need—if you've marked incorrectly, you can always make the hole bigger, but if you've cut it too big, you need to start over with a new bag.)

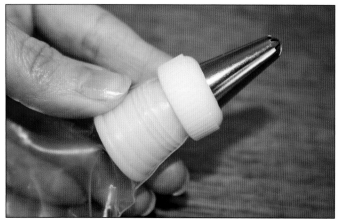

Take the coupler and tip out and cut along where you've marked. Slide them back in to check. Keep adjusting as necessary, until your tip fits through the hole, but the coupler doesn't. Attach your ring, and move on to filling your bag.

How to Fill a Piping Bag

Hold your piping bag in your off-hand (I'm right-handed, so I hold it in my left hand) close to the tip.

Roll the bag down over your hand.

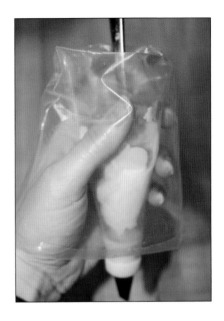

Spoon frosting into the bag, trying to get it as close to the tip as possible.

Use the hand holding the bag to squeeze the frosting off the spoon.

Once you have enough frosting in the bag, roll the bag off your hand, and squeeze the frosting down toward the tip.

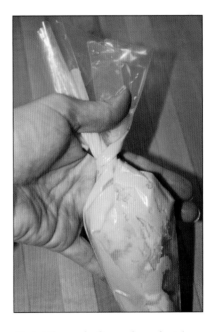

Twist the end of your bag shut (you can also use a rubber band, or buy a little clamp that will hold it shut for you—though I still recommend twisting it just to be safe), and push all the air out of your bag.

Holding the Piping Bag

Once you've twisted the piping bag shut, sit the twist of the bag between the thumb and forefinger of your writing hand.

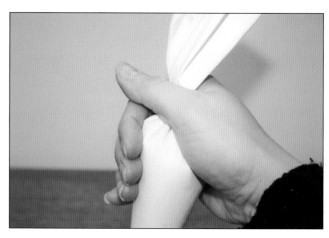

Close your hand around the bag.

You can now squeeze and steer the bag with one hand. (For better accuracy, steer from your shoulder, using your whole arm, rather than just using your wrist.) If you don't find this gives you enough control, you can always use your left hand to help steer at the tip. I often use a two-handed grip when my piping bag is full.

There are two basic angles to hold the piping bag at:
- 90°—the bag is straight up and down, perpendicular to the cake.
- 45°—the bag is held at a 45° angle, tipped in the direction you are piping.

Springing a Leak

Every so often, piping bags pop, and frosting comes oozing out of all the wrong places. This may happen for a few reasons:

1. Your tip is clogged—if you've been squeezing and squeezing and getting nowhere, chances are some butter or margarine has clogged up your tip. Remove the tip, clean it out with a skewer or toothpick, or soak it in hot water to clear the clog, and move on to repairing or replacing your bag.

2. Your frosting is too thick—if your tip isn't clogged, but you're still doing way more squeezing than piping, your frosting is probably too thick. Scoop it out (sometimes you can remove the tip and squeeze it out through the coupler) into a bowl and thin the frosting according to the directions in the Checking Your Consistency section of this book.

3. Your tip popped out—this only happens if you weren't using a coupler. Sometimes the pressure is enough to stretch the bag and let the tip slip out. If this happens, you'll need to get a new bag.

4. Your bag is worn out—sadly, piping bags don't last forever. Coupling rings exert a fair bit of wear and tear. It's possible your bag has just worn through.

If you're using a disposable piping bag or a plastic bag, you may be able to save it with an application of tape. Simply wipe the area off with a paper towel to remove the greasy residue and stick the tape over the hole. Unfortunately, if you're using a reusable bag, it probably means the bag has worn thin and you will need to replace it with a new one.

Cleaning Your Piping Bags and Tips

Once the cake is done, all that's left is cleaning up. Detach your tips and coupler from the bag. Empty out all the leftover frosting, and rinse the bag with hot water.

Soak your tips in hot, soapy water (a small bowl or cup will do) to help clear out the packed-in frosting.

Turn your bag inside out and drizzle dish soap over the bag. Massage the soap over and around the bag. Rinse well with hot water. Stand it up over a utensil to dry.

Emptied-out tips may be washed in the top rack of your dishwasher (if you have a mesh bag to keep them in)—personally, I found this discolored mine, so I use a soapy cloth and/or my tip brush (a bottle brush will do), then rinse with hot water.

PIPING 101

The following techniques range from simple lines to more complex designs like roses and basketweave. With a steady hand and a little practice, you'll be frosting up creative confections in no time!

Simple Lines
(Tips #1, 2, 3, 5, and 12)
Lines are probably the simplest things to pipe. Lines are used for vines, outlining, smiles, and many other designs in this book.

Note: The size of your tip will determine the width of your lines, but with all tips, the harder you squeeze, the thicker your line will be.

Hold your bag at a 45° angle, just above the surface of the cake. Gently squeeze the bag until some frosting comes out and touches the cake, anchoring it there. In a smooth motion, move your piping bag to the right for right-handed people, to the left for lefties, while squeezing.

When you reach the end of your line, release pressure on the bag and pull the bag away.

If the end of your line sticks up away from the cake, use a toothpick or skewer to gently push it back in place.

Dots
(Tips #1, 2, 3, 5, and 12)
Dots are also used quite frequently in this book. Dots are used as flower centers, eyes, borders, and more.

Note: Dots can be made larger than the width of your tip by simply squeezing out more frosting before you release pressure and pull away, but generally speaking, the larger the tip size, the larger the dot.

Simple Dots

Hold your bag at a 90° angle, just above the surface of the cake.

Squeeze the bag until the dot reaches the size you want, press down slightly as you release pressure, then pull away.

If part of your dot sticks up, use a toothpick or your finger to gently press it back into place.

Dot Borders
(Tip #12)

Dot borders are a simple way to give the base of your cake (where it meets the plate), a smooth, finished look.

Hold your bag at a 90° angle, with the bag pointing away from the cake. Squeeze the bag until the dot is about the size of a chickpea. Release pressure as you gently press into the dot. Pull the bag away.

Move your bag over about a ¼ inch and pipe another dot, exactly the same size as the last. Repeat until you have a full border of dots around your entire cake.

If any dots stick up, use your finger or a toothpick to gently press the frosting back into place.

Stars
(Tips: small #16, medium #18, large #21, extra-large #1M,
Triple-Star tip—which seems to have no number that I can find)

Stars can be used as a border around edges, to fill in outlines, or on their own as a decoration. When filling in large outlines, use the Triple Star tip to cover more space faster.

Hold your piping bag at a 90° angle, just above the cake. Squeeze the bag. When the star reaches the size you want, release pressure and pull bag away.

Shell borders
(Star tips: small #16, medium #18, large #21, extra-large #1M)

A simple yet elegant way to conceal messy cake edges, shell borders can be used at the base of the cake (where it meets the serving plate) and on the top edge.

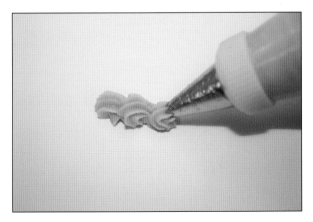

Hold your piping bag at a 45° angle, just above the cake. Squeeze hard, lifting your bag up and away from you, letting the frosting balloon out.

In a fluid motion, pull the bag down and toward you while reducing pressure. Repeat without stopping, until your border goes all the way around your cake.

Simple Flowers

(Small: #225, Large: #2D)

Put frosting in a piping bag with one of your flower tips.

Hold your piping bag at a 90° angle just above the cake.

Squeeze gently, at the same time twisting your wrist about a quarter turn—this will fan out the frosting into petals. Don't go too far, or you'll just end up with a smeary mess. Release pressure on the bag and pull away.

Pipe a yellow dot in the center of each flower, or place one silver or gold dragee there.

Grass and Hair

(Tip #233)

A simple tip to use. The only difference between piping grass and hair is the angle at which you hold your piping bag.

Grass and Short, Spiky Hair

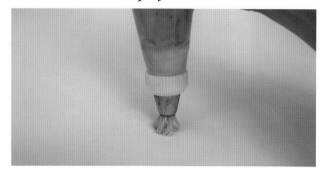

Hold your bag at a 90° angle, just above the surface of the cake. Squeeze the bag in a quick burst, then release pressure and pull it away.

Move the tip into an empty space beside the piped grass/hair and repeat. Continue piping grass until you have covered the whole surface you want to have grass/hair on.

Writing

(Tips #1, 2, 3, and 5)

Writing on cakes is about as easy as writing on paper—only you get to use frosting instead of pencils.

The trickiest part of writing on cakes (for me, at least) is getting the words centered. The best trick I have found is to write the words out on a piece of paper the size you would like them on the cake. Hold the paper over the cake (be careful not to touch it to the cake) and center the words, then make a small mark with a toothpick or skewer to tell you where to write.

Still not sure you can do it? There's nothing wrong with using a toothpick or skewer to lightly sketch the words onto the cake. Then, all you have to do is trace over top of them with your frosting.

Handwriting not the best? You can buy a set of cake alphabet stamps at most cake stores, or use clean ink stamps to imprint your words into the cake and simply trace over top with the frosting.

Printed Letters

Piping printed letters is as easy as piping lines.

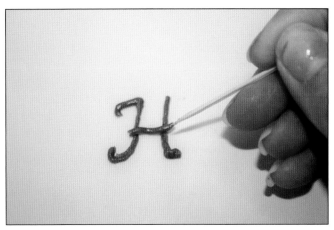

Hold your bag at a 45° angle, with your bag pointing to the right. Your tip should be just above the surface of the cake. Pipe each line using your line technique in the same order you would print the letter on paper—this technique is the same for fancy printed (not joined) letters as it is for plain printing.

If the ends of lines stick up, use a toothpick or skewer to gently press them back down onto the cake.

Cursive Letters

Piping cursive letters is also very similar to writing them on paper.

Hold your bag at a 45° angle, with your bag pointing to the right. Your tip should be just above the surface of the cake.

Squeeze the bag, letting a small amount of frosting come out and stick to the cake. In a smooth motion, while squeezing, move the bag to pipe the letters. At the end of each word, release pressure on the bag and pull it away. Move over to the next spot and begin piping the next word.

The trick here is to keep consistent pressure on the bag the entire time you are piping. If you squeeze harder at any point, your line will get thicker. If you release pressure too early, your line will stop, effectively breaking the word. If that happens, place your tip as close as you can to the broken spot and resume piping. Use a toothpick or skewer when you are finished to gently attach the two frosting threads to each other. And remember, frosting is about as permanent as pencil—if all else fails, scrape it off (you'll probably need to flat-ice over the spot) and re-pipe your word on top.

Basketweave
(Tip #47)

Basketweave looks very complex, but it's actually a very simple technique to do. When you're done, your guests won't be able to tell your cake from a real basket.

Hold your piping bag at a 45° angle with the smooth side of the tip facing away from the cake (serrated side facing the cake).

Squeeze the bag and let some frosting come out and stick to the cake. In a smooth motion, while squeezing, move the bag in a straight line up to the top of the cake. Release pressure and pull bag away.

Turn the bag so the serrated side of the tip is facing away from the cake. Starting at the top of the cake, hold the bag about ¼ inch to one side of the plain line you just piped, and pipe a serrated line across the plain line.

Move your bag down, leaving a space the width of piping tip between the line you just piped and the line you are going to pipe. Pipe another serrated line across the plain line. Continue piping serrated lines until you run out of cake (it's okay if the last line doesn't touch the bottom).

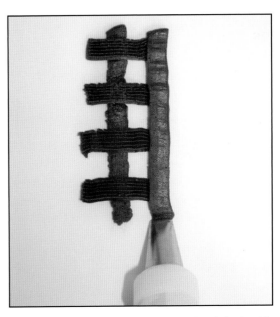

Hold your piping bag at a 45° angle, right beside the end of the serrated lines. Pipe a plain line up the side of the cake, touching the ends of the serrated lines.

Turn your bag so the serrated side of the piping tip is facing away from the cake. Hold your bag at a 45° angle in the first empty space between serrated lines. Pipe a serrated line from beside your original plain line, across the new plain line, about ¼ inch past the new line.

Continue filling in the empty spaces between serrated lines, by piping new serrated lines from the first plain line, across the new plain line, until you have reached the last empty space.

Turn your bag so the plain side faces away from the cake. Pipe a plain line up the side of the cake, touching the edges of the last column of serrated lines. Hold your bag at a 45° angle in the first empty space between serrated lines. Pipe a serrated line from beside your original plain line, across the new plain line, about ¼ inch past the new line.

Continue piping new plain lines, and filling in the spaces between the serrated lines by piping new serrated lines over the newest plain lines, until you have completed your basket.

Lattice

A lattice uses the same basic technique as the basketweave, only spaced out more across the cake. This technique is used to reproduce a pie lattice in the Pretend Pie design on page 65. Unlike the basketweave, you should keep the serrated edge of the tip always facing toward the cake, so all the lines are plain.

Start by piping a long line down the length of your cake.

Pipe two 2-inch-long lines across the first line, about two inches away from each other.

Pipe another line up and down, just overlapping the ends of your two-inch lines.

Pipe a line from the side of the first up and down line, across the second, ending about one inch away from the second up and down line.

Continue alternating two-inch-long lines, spaced two inches apart, until you have covered your cake in a lattice pattern.

Scales

(Cupcake-filling tip #230)

Useful for dragons, snakes, or even fish, scales take time to pipe, but in my opinion, the look is worth the effort.

Place your cupcake-filling tip into a piping bag with frosting, and hold it at a 90° angle to your cake. Squeeze the bag as you pull the bag to the side—this will drag the tip through the frosting as you pipe, flattening it into a scale shape. Each scale should be about ¼-inch long, and sit tightly next to the scales on either side.

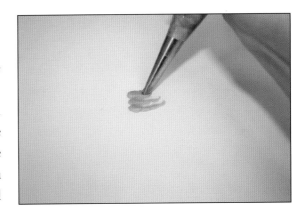

Bricklay Pattern

All scales, be they piped or made of candy, should be laid out in a bricklay pattern. A bricklay pattern uses multiple rows, lined up just offset from each other so each scale sits between two scales from the row under it.

Roses

(Tips #12 + #103)

Would a frosting rose by any other name taste as sweet? Probably, but they're still fun to make.

Note: Roses require a stiff consistency frosting to hold their shape.

To make roses for full-sized cakes, you will need some wax or parchment papers (as many 2-inch parchment squares as roses) and something to stick them to. Ideally I would suggest you purchase a "rose nail" from a baking/craft store. They only cost a few dollars and are specifically designed for making frosting roses. If, however, you don't want to invest in something you won't use very often, you can substitute an upside down drinking glass with a flat bottom or a small bowl—something that fits comfortably in your hand, so you can turn it as you work.

You may make cupcake roses directly on the cupcakes themselves—simply substitute the word *paper* in the instructions below for the word *cupcake*.

Start with your large round tip (#12) on your piping bag. Use a small piece of tape or sticky tack to attach your wax/parchment paper square to your rose nail or bottom of a glass. You can also use a small dot of frosting, but it doesn't always stick well enough.

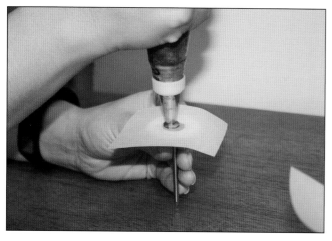

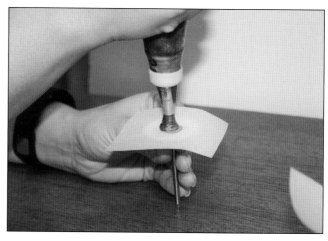

Hold your bag at a 90° angle, just above the surface of the paper. Squeeze the piping bag hard. Letting the frosting balloon out a bit.

In a smooth motion, slowly reduce pressure on the bag as you pull up and away from the paper.

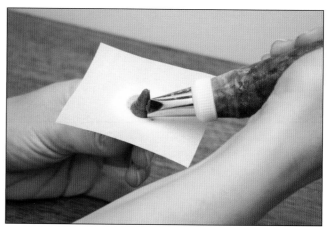

Release pressure entirely, and pull bag away. You should now have a frosting cone on the paper that sits about ½ inch tall.

Switch to your petal tip (#103). Hold your bag at a 45° angle to the cone, with the larger opening of the tip facing down.

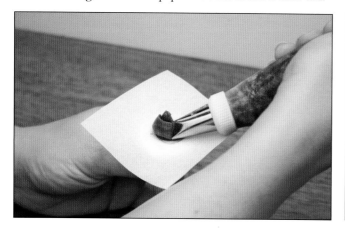

Squeeze the bag and turn your wrist away from you, while turning the nail or glass in the opposite direction, wrapping a frosting "petal" around half of the cone.

Repeat one or two more times, starting each new petal overlapping the end of the previous petal, until you have several petals wrapped around the cone.

Change the position of the bag, so you are now holding it at a 90° angle from the cone—your tip should be pointing straight at the cone, and the bag lying parallel to the wax/parchment paper.

Squeeze the bag while moving the bag away from you, at the same time turning the nail/glass toward you. Each new petal should start overlapping the end of the previous petal. Continue working your way outward until you reach your desired rose size.

Remove the wax/parchment paper square carefully from the nail/glass, and sit it somewhere flat to let the rose harden. Note: the buttercream recipe in this book stiffens into a crust, but doesn't go rock-hard like the ones you can buy in cake stores (those use royal icing, which is durable but not at all tasty), so you'll have to handle your roses with care.

For larger roses (especially those on cupcakes), you can squeeze your bag faster than you turn, allowing your petals to create a ruffle effect, and fill in the space better.

Once the roses have stiffened (I'd wait at least an hour), you can carefully use your frosting spatula to gently lift them off the wax/parchment paper and onto your cake. If you made the rose directly on a cupcake, no more work is needed.

Practice is definitely the key to getting your roses perfect. The good news is, you can always scrape off imperfect ones (before they stiffen) and stick the frosting back in the piping bag—just try not to re-use your frosting too much, as the heat from your hands can cause it to break after repeated use.

Fill in the Blanks

Perhaps the easiest way to re-create a picture on top of a cake is to draw an outline, and then fill in the image with one of your star tips (#16, #18, #21, or the Triple Star—depending on the size of the image).

There are two basic ways to create your outline:

1. Use a cookie cutter—gently press a cookie cutter into your cake where you want the image to appear. Remove it, and fill in the spaces with one of your star tips. An example of this technique can be seen in the Clever Cookie Cutter design on page 57.

2. Reverse image transfer—this one requires a few steps, but can be used to re-create sports logos, character emblems, or even coloring book pages. Start by printing off a reverse image of your design—most computer programs allow you to flip the image. *This is important, as the design will come out as a mirror image of what is on your paper.*

   Lay a piece of wax or parchment paper on top of the design, and trace it with piping gel. (White gel is available at most grocery stores, while clear gel can be found in the baking department of most craft stores.)

   Flip the wax or parchment paper over onto a flat-iced cake, and gently smooth your hand over top, lightly pressing the gel onto the cake.

   Carefully peel off the wax or parchment paper. The gel design should stay in on the cake. Use one of your star tips to fill in the blank spaces with the appropriate colors.

   This technique is illustrated in the Simple Starburst design on page 61.

DECORATING ACCENTS

There are so many fun things you can add to frosted cakes and cupcakes to make them even more spectacular. This section will give a quick run-down of all the wonderful treats you can use to make your cakes stand out.

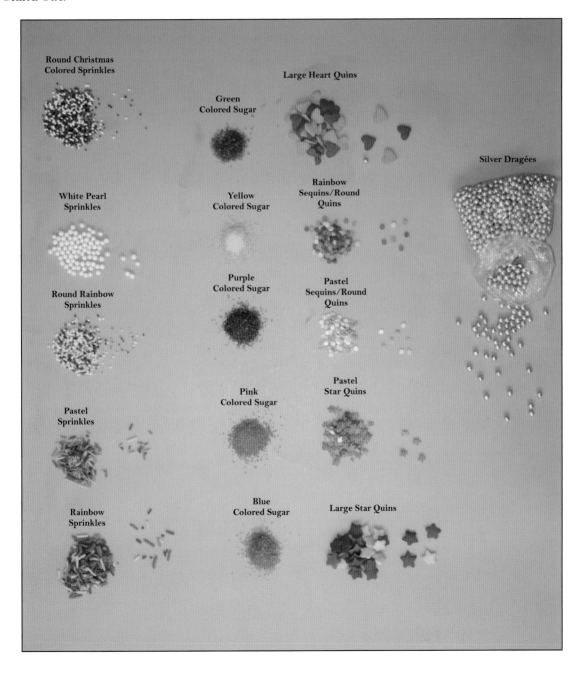

Sprinkles, Sugars, Quins, and Dragées

Typically sold by the jarful, these traditional cake decorations are the perfect finishing touch for cupcakes.

Sprinkles

These small sugary bits of color make any cake fun. The term *sprinkles* covers both the rainbow and pastel cylinders, and the tiny round beads sold in rainbow and Christmas colors, as well as larger colored pearls.

The cylinder sprinkles are typically sold in a jar of mixed colors, but some bulk-candy stores allow you to buy them by color—meaning you can create your own custom sprinkle mix, be it red and yellow for your favorite sports team, or blue, purple, and white for a frosty, ice-themed party.

Sugars

Simply colored coarse sugar, these little sweeties add sparkle to cakes and cupcakes alike. You can buy these by the jar, or color your own by mixing a few drops of food coloring into a small bag of coarse sugar and blending well. This same technique can be used to color coconut, as well.

Quins

Also available by the jar, sugar quins come in lots of shapes and colors. The small round quins (also called sequins) and star quins are available in bright rainbow colors as well as pastels to brighten up cupcakes, while shapes such as cows, dinosaurs, and dolphins come only in their theme colors. You can also find jars of large stars, hearts, and other shapes to add style to larger cakes.

Dragées

These gold and silver balls are the perfect touch of glitter for your cakes. Whether using them as flower centers, snowflake sparkles, or robot rivets, the hint of shiny sugar will be just the accent your cake needs.

Candy

Mmm . . . candy. Not only is it sweet and tasty, it makes great cake decorations. Whether you're using a single gummy butterfly as a cupcake topper, or using licorice laces as balloon strings, candies play a major part in most of the designs in this book.

If you're using just a few candies on your cake, I suggest buying some extras and putting them out in a bowl when it's time to serve—it helps cut down on battles over who gets which candy when the cake is cut.

Note: If you can't find Hot Lips, use a tube of red Decorator's Icing and the large round (#12) compatible tip and pipe a smile/lips on your cake.

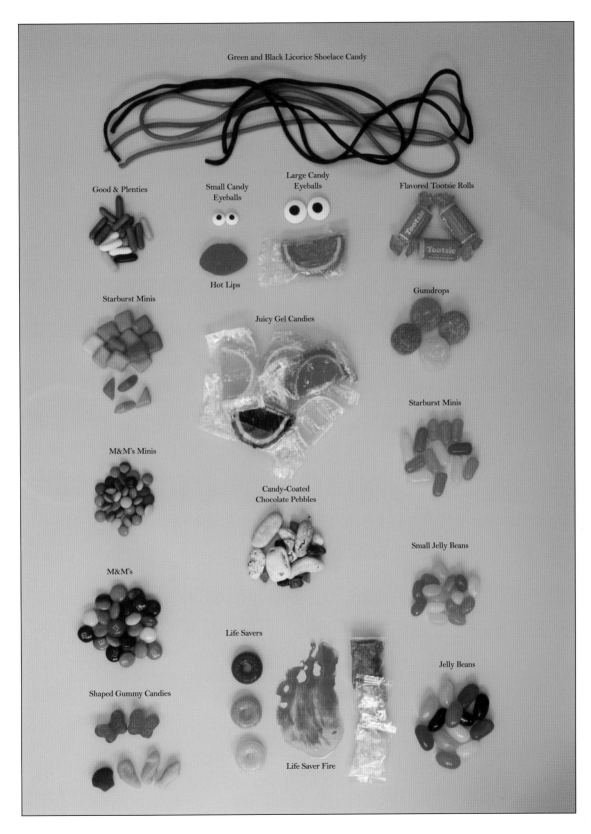

Green and Black Licorice Shoelace Candy

Good & Plenties

Small Candy Eyeballs

Large Candy Eyeballs

Flavored Tootsie Rolls

Hot Lips

Starburst Minis

Juicy Gel Candies

Gumdrops

M&M's Minis

Candy-Coated Chocolate Pebbles

Starburst Minis

M&M's

Small Jelly Beans

Life Savers

Jelly Beans

Shaped Gummy Candies

Life Saver Fire

Life Saver Fire

Life Savers are a fun treat that can function as buttons and eyes, but they have another use, too: fire.

To make Life Saver fire, preheat your oven to 350°F. Crush yellow, red, and orange Life Savers using a heavy utensil (the back of a blunt knife works well).

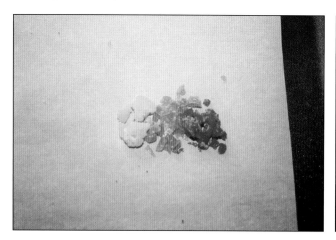 

Line a cookie sheet with parchment paper, and lay out two or three groups of crushed yellow Life Savers. Place some crushed orange Life Savers next to each pile of yellow. Place crushed red Life Savers next to each pile of orange.

As soon as you get them out of the oven, use a wavy motion to run a fork through the groups of Life Savers, going from yellow to red.

Bake in the oven for 2–3 minutes, watching—you want to pull them out when they melt, before they start to bubble.

Let them cool until hardened. Place them on your cake at the last moment before serving or displaying (otherwise the Life Savers will absorb moisture from the cake and begin to melt).

Miscellaneous

I love finding new tasty treats to decorate my cakes. Colored coconut, melting wafers, graham crackers, chocolate bars, fruit snacks, and cookies are just some of the delicious additions to the designs in this book.

Edible Sand

Edible sand is my own recipe, and it's as easy to make as it is tasty. Simply combine equal parts graham cracker crumbs and brown sugar and sprinkle over a flat-iced cake. Best served on chocolate cakes filled with Gooey Marshmallow Filling for a yummy s'mores-esque treat.

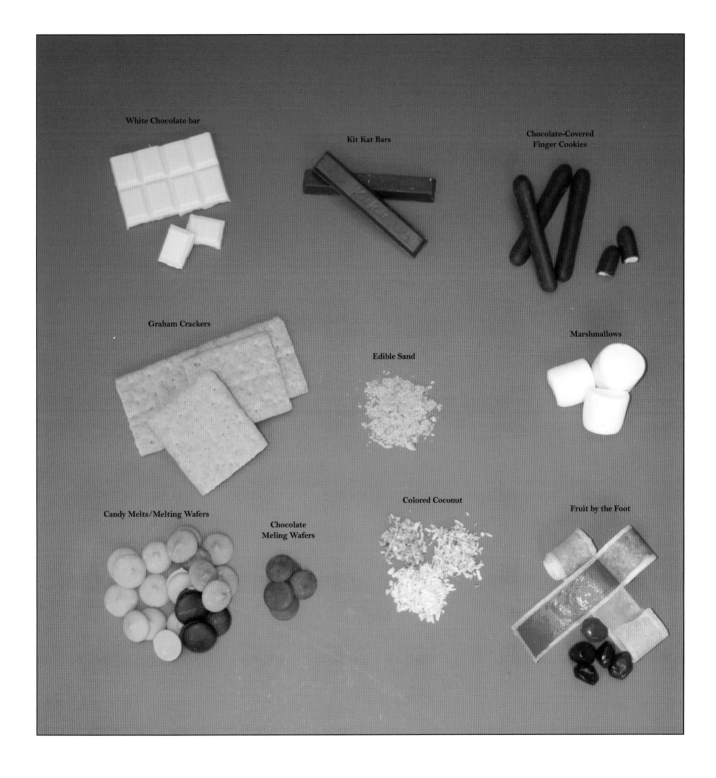

RELIABLE RECIPES

CAKES

The following cake recipes are my favorite, most reliable recipes. All of them work great as layer cakes, cupcakes, or cakeballs, but only the Pound Cake recipe and the Cake Mix Fix are sturdy enough to hold up to the carving required for the Creative Cutout designs (page 169).

All cake recipes can be made dairy-free by substituting water, or soy/coconut/almond/rice milk for milk, and your favorite non-dairy cream cheese (softened) for yogurt.

Unfortunately, I have yet to find a really good gluten-free cake recipe, but there are some excellent mixes out there. Substituting an equal amount of club soda for the called-for liquid in one of those mixes will give you a denser, richer, dairy-free, egg-free, gluten-free cake.

For more information on baking tools, tips and techniques, check out the Baking section of this book (page 1).

All recipes yield enough batter for the designs in this book—however, some pans (especially loaf pans) vary greatly in size. Pans shouldn't be filled more than two-thirds full, or they could bubble over, oozing batter into the oven. If your pans can't hold all the batter, I suggest using the extra for a batch of cupcakes.

Pound Cake
- 1 cup butter
- 2 cups sugar
- ¾ cup plain Greek yogurt
- 2 cups flour
- 4 eggs
- 1½ teaspoons vanilla extract

Method
Preheat your oven to 325°F. (I make this in my stand mixer, but you could use an electric hand mixer or manual whisk.) Cream together butter and sugar. Beat in yogurt. Alternate adding flour and eggs. Add vanilla and beat thoroughly (about two minutes on medium). Pour into greased and floured pans.

Bake 25 to 35 minutes for 8-inch pans, 25 to 30 minutes for 9 x 13-inch pan, 20 to 25 minutes for 9-inch pie plates, 30 to 40 minutes for small metal mixing bowls, 15 to 20 minutes for cupcakes, 20 to 25 minutes for bundt pans, and 5 minutes for cakeballs.

Pound Cake Variations

- Lemon Pound Cake: Replace vanilla with 1 teaspoon lemon juice + 1 tablespoon grated lemon rind.
- Lemon-Raspberry Pound Cake*: Replace vanilla with 1 teaspoon lemon juice + 1 tablespoon grated lemon rind. Stir in 1 cup fresh or frozen raspberries.
- Orange Pound Cake: Replace vanilla with 1 teaspoon orange juice + 1 tablespoon grated orange rind.
- Almond Pound Cake: Replace vanilla with 1 teaspoon almond extract.
- Cherry-Almond Pound Cake*: Replace vanilla with 1 teaspoon almond extract. Stir in 1 cup diced, pitted fresh cherries *or* diced candied cherries.
- Chocolate Pound Cake: Add ½ cup cocoa powder.

*Cakes with added chunks of fruit are not stable enough for carving.

Chocolate Cake

- 2 cups chocolate milk (or 2 cups milk + 2 tablespoons chocolate powder or syrup)
- ¼ cup cocoa powder
- 1 cup butter/hard margarine
- 2 eggs
- 2 cups brown sugar
- ⅛ teaspoon salt
- 2 teaspoons vanilla extract
- 2 cups flour
- 1 teaspoon baking powder
- 2 teaspoons baking soda dissolved in 2 tablespoons milk

Method

Preheat oven to 350°F. Heat the milk and cocoa in a saucepan on medium heat, stirring constantly, until thickened (about 5 minutes). Remove from heat. Add the butter, and let the mixture sit to melt it in (about 5 minutes). Whisk the mixture and add eggs, stirring constantly. Add brown sugar, salt, vanilla, flour, and baking powder. Mix well. Stir in baking soda-milk mixture. Beat well—until all lumps disappear.

Pour into greased and floured pans. Bake 25 to 35 minutes for 8-inch pans, 25 to 30 minutes for a 9 x 13-inch pan, 20 to 25 minutes for 9-inch pie plates, 30 to 35 minutes for small metal mixing bowls, 10 to 15 minutes for cupcakes, 20 to 25 minutes for bundt pans, and 5 minutes for cakeballs.

Pink Lemonade Cake

- ½ cup shortening
- ¼ cup hard margarine or butter, softened
- 1¾ cups sugar
- 3 eggs
- 2½ cups flour
- 2½ teaspoons baking powder
- dash salt
- 1 cup pink lemonade concentrate, thawed
- ¼ cup water

Method

Preheat oven to 375°F. Cream together the shortening, butter/margarine, and sugar with an electric or stand mixer. Add the eggs, one at a time. In a separate bowl, stir together flour, baking powder, and salt. Alternate adding flour mixture and lemonade concentrate to the butter-sugar-egg mixture. Beat well until the batter is smooth.

Pour into greased, floured pans and bake 25 to 35 minutes for 8-inch pans, 25 to 30 minutes for 9 x 13-inch pan, 20 to 25 minutes for 9-inch pie plates, 30 to 35 minutes for small metal mixing bowls, 10 to 15 minutes for cupcakes, 20 to 25 minutes for bundt pans, and 5 minutes for cakeballs.

Cake Mix Fix

- 1 box cake mix
- ⅓ cup butter or hard margarine, softened
- 3 eggs
- 1 cup vanilla Greek yogurt or 1 cup plain Greek yogurt + 1 teaspoon vanilla

Method

Preheat oven to 350°F. Combine ingredients and beat well (batter will be thick). Pour into floured, greased pans. Bake 25 to 35 minutes for 8-inch pans, 25 to 30 minutes for 9 x 13-inch pan, 20 to 25 minutes for 9-inch pie plates, 30 to 40 minutes for small metal mixing bowls, 15 to 20 minutes for cupcakes, 20 to 25 minutes for bundt pans, and 5 minutes for cakeballs.

FILLINGS

These are my favorite, most reliable fillings. All three fillings are naturally gluten-free. The Raspberry is also dairy-free, while the Dark Chocolate Ganache and Gooey Marshmallow Fillings have dairy-free variations.

For more about filling tips and techniques, see the Filling section of this book (page 6).

Dark Chocolate Ganache
- 4 ounces dark chocolate, coarsely chopped, or 4 ounces semisweet chocolate chips
- 4 ounces whipping cream

Method
Coarsely chop your chocolate and set it aside. Heat the whipping cream in a small saucepan over medium heat, stirring constantly until it just starts to boil. Remove it from the heat. Add the coarsely chopped chocolate/chocolate chips. *Do not stir.* Let it sit for 10 minutes.

Gently stir in the chocolate until blended. Let it sit another 10 minutes, or until it has set enough to spread on your cake.

Ganache can be made in advance and stored in the refrigerator for 3 days, or the freezer for up to 3 months. Bring up to room temperature, or heat slightly in microwave to make spreadable.

Ganache Variations
- Dairy-Free Dark Chocolate Ganache: Replace whipping cream with 4 ounces full-fat coconut milk. Make sure to use dairy-free dark chocolate.
- Milk Chocolate Ganache: Replace chopped dark chocolate with 7 ounces chopped milk chocolate.
- White Chocolate Ganache: Replace chopped dark chocolate with 7 ounces chopped white chocolate.
- Yogurt Ganache: Okay, this one might not "technically" be a ganache, but replace the chopped dark chocolate with 7 ounces yogurt chips for a tangy, cream cheese–like filling.

Gooey Marshmallow Filling

- ¼ cup whipping cream
- 1 teaspoon sugar
- ½ teaspoon vanilla
- ½ cup marshmallow creme
- 3 cups powdered/confectioner's/icing sugar

Method

Whip cream, sugar, and vanilla together until stiff peaks form. Add marshmallow creme and beat on low. Add sugar slowly and continue to beat on low until mixture is fully combined.

Variation

- Dairy-Free Gooey Marshmallow Filling: use ¼ cup coconut cream instead of whipping cream.

Raspberry Filling

- 1 cup raspberries (fresh or frozen—no need to thaw)
- 1 tablespoon water
- ¼ cup sugar
- 1 tablespoon cornstarch dissolved in ⅛ cup water

Method

Pour raspberries and 1 tablespoon water into saucepan (the water should cover the bottom of saucepan) and simmer, covered, on medium heat for 10 minutes.

Add sugar and stir until dissolved. Reduce to low heat and continue simmering until the raspberries break down into sauce (about 10 to 15 minutes), stirring occasionally. Stir in cornstarch and water mixture, and simmer another 10 minutes. Remove from heat and cool before using.

Raspberry filling can be stored in the fridge for up to 3 days, and in the freezer for up to 3 months.

FROSTINGS

The following recipes are my favorite, most reliable frosting recipes. All of them work well for flat-icing and filling cakes, but only the Basic Buttercream Frosting recipe (including all of its variations) is designed for piping.

All of the frosting recipes are naturally gluten-free and can be made dairy-free by using dairy-free margarine or shortening instead of butter.

For more about frosting tools, tips, and techniques, see the Frosting section of this book (page 13).

Basic Buttercream
- ½ cup butter or hard margarine*
- ½ cup shortening*
- 4 tablespoons water**
- 1¼ teaspoons vanilla flavoring
- 4 cups icing/powdered/confectioner's sugar
- dash of salt (less than ⅛ teaspoon)

Method
Cream wet ingredients until mixed. Add sugar and salt and beat until blended.

*Tips on selecting the right fat can be found on page 15.
** 4 tablespoons of water = thin consistency, 2 tablespoons = thick consistency, 3 tablespoons = medium consistency—all designs in this book take thin consistency unless otherwise indicated.

Variations
- Almond Buttercream: Replace vanilla with ¾ teaspoon almond extract.
- Mint Buttercream: Replace vanilla with 1–1½ teaspoons peppermint extract.
- Chocolate Buttercream (better for piping): Add ½ cup cocoa powder and 1 tablespoon water to Basic Buttercream recipe.
- Lemon Buttercream: Replace vanilla with 1 teaspoon lemon extract or replace vanilla with 1 tablespoon lemon juice and reduce water by 1 tablespoon.

Fudgy Chocolate Frosting

- ½ cup butter or margarine, melted
- ½ teaspoon vanilla extract
- ⅓ cup water
- 3 cups confectioner's/powdered/icing sugar

Method

Mix together melted butter, vanilla, and water. Stir in sugar. This is perfect for flat-icing.

Variation

- Creamy Chocolate-Mint Frosting: Substitute ½ teaspoon peppermint extract for the ½ teaspoon vanilla.

Dreamy Cream Cheese Frosting

- ¼ cup butter or margarine
- 1 teaspoon vanilla extract
- 3 cups confectioner's/powdered/icing sugar
- 8 ounces hard cream cheese, cubed

Method

Cream butter/margarine, vanilla, and sugar together. Slowly add cubes of cream cheese and beat until fully mixed. This one is also perfect for flat-icing.

Variation

- Lemon Cream Cheese Frosting: Replace ½ teaspoon vanilla with 1 teaspoon lemon juice.

DELIGHTFUL DESIGNS

2-D TREATS

The designs in this section are the simplest to make and an excellent start for beginner decorators. They combine flat-icing and simple piping techniques on basic cake shapes to create fun cakes for all ages.

TRADITIONAL YET TRENDY

These days, birthday cake is one of the hottest flavors out there; you can get birthday cake–flavored pancakes, ice cream, and even lattes, so it seems fitting the first design in the book is a throw-back to the cake that started it all: the traditional birthday cake.

You Will Need:
- 1 recipe vanilla Pound Cake (page 41), baked as two 8-inch round layers
- 1 recipe vanilla Basic Buttercream (page 46)
- small bowl
- blue food coloring
- 2 piping bags
- 2 couplers and rings
- large star tip (#21)
- small round tip (#3)
- 2 tablespoons rainbow sprinkles
- 2 tablespoons rainbow quins

How to Decorate Traditional Yet Trendy Birthday Cake

Scoop 1 cup Basic Buttercream into a small bowl and tint it pale blue. Put the frosting into a piping bag with a coupler and the small round tip (#3) and set it aside.

Level both cakes and sit the bottom cake cut-side down on a serving plate.

Scoop 1 cup white Basic Buttercream into a piping bag with a coupler and the large star tip (#21). Pipe a dam along the outside edge of the top of the bottom layer of cake.

Spread a thick layer of white frosting inside the dam. Assemble the cake, then crumb-coat and flat-ice it with white frosting.

Using the piping bag of blue frosting, pipe the words *Happy Birthday* on top of the cake.

Using the piping bag of white frosting, pipe a shell border on the top edge of the cake—this will help hide the edge, which is the hardest part to get smooth.

Carefully scatter sprinkles over the shell border—you want to try and keep them contained to the shell border. If any land on the sides of the cake or on the cake plate, simply pick them off with your fingers or tweezers.

Press rainbow quins one at a time into the sides of the cake in a scattered formation to look like falling confetti—these will help disguise any places where sprinkles were picked out.

Use the piping bag of blue frosting to pipe a shell border around the bottom edge of the cake (where it meets the serving plate).

CLASSIC CUPCAKES

These cupcakes are simple to make, but beautiful to look at. Top with fruit or frosting flowers for a sophisticated look, or candy, sprinkles, or quins for a festive feel.

You Will Need:
- 1 cake recipe, baked as 24 cupcakes
- 1 recipe Basic Buttercream *(stiff consistency)* (page 46)
- piping bag
- coupler or extra-large star tip (#1M) or large flower tip (#2D)
- your choice of topper: sprinkles, quins, sugar, fruit, or frosting flowers—frosting flowers require large flower tip (#2D), ½ cup colored frosting, and 24 silver dragées

How to Decorate Classic Cupcakes
There are three main styles of frosting on cupcakes: ruffles, spirals, and coils—the only difference between the three is the tip used to pipe them.

Ruffles   **Spiral**   **Coil**

A ruffle frosting uses the large flower tip (#2D), a spiral top uses the large star tip (#1M), and a coil top uses just a coupler, without a tip.

Personally, I find the ruffle and spiral frosting styles the easiest—the coil top needs to be perfectly circular, and you have to make sure the notch in the coupler is always facing in. Also, unless you want your cupcakes looking like a certain stinky emoji, I wouldn't use the coil top with chocolate frosting.

For all tops, fill your piping bag with about 1 cup of frosting (you will need to refill—these take a surprising amount of frosting) along with your appropriate tip/coupler.

Hold the bag at a 90° angle and start at the outside edge.

Squeeze the piping bag and work your way around the outside edge, moving inward in a spiraling motion, building the frosting up on top of itself.

When you get to the center, release pressure as you pull away, finishing the topper in a peak.

The key to getting perfect cupcake toppers is practice. The good news? If you have a cupcake topper you don't like, simply scrape off the frosting and try again. So long as there are no crumbs in your frosting, you can even pop it back into your piping bag and re-use it—just be careful of re-using it too many times, as the heat from your hands can cause the frosting to break.

Once complete, gently press your topper or sprinkle your sprinkles onto the still-wet frosting so they will stick better.

For frosting flower toppers, you want to let the frosting form a crust (wait about 10 minutes) and use a finger to gently flatten a spot on top of your frosting to hold the flower. For instructions on piping frosting flowers, see the Simple Flowers directions on page 26.

CLEVER COOKIE CUTTER

This cake uses a simple cookie cutter to create an adorable giraffe cake that almost anyone can make.

You Will Need:
- 1 cake recipe, baked as two 8-inch round layers
- 1 recipe Basic Buttercream (page 46)
- 1 recipe filling of your choice (or use some of your Basic Buttercream)
- green, yellow, and red food coloring
- 2 small bowls
- 2 piping bags
- small star tip (#16)
- medium star tip (#21)
- giraffe cookie cutter
- 1 tube Black Decorator's Icing*
- 1 small round tip (#3) compatible with Decorator's Icing*

*Since these are just used for the giraffe's eye, you could substitute a green or blue quin for the eye and not bother with the Decorator's Icing.

How to Decorate Clever Cookie Cutter Cake

Scoop ½ cup Basic Buttercream into a small bowl and tint it yellow. Cover it and set it aside.

Scoop ½ cup Basic Buttercream into a small bowl and tint it pale orange using red and yellow food coloring. Set it aside.

Tint the remaining frosting pale green. Place 1 cup green frosting into a piping bag with the medium star tip (#21).

Level your cakes. Use the green frosting in the piping bag to pipe a dam around the bottom layer. Spread your desired filling inside the dam. Assemble the cake, and use the green frosting to crumb-coat and flat-ice it.

Decide on the best side of your cake—this should be the side that looks the flattest, with the smoothest frosting. Turn the cake so that side points toward you.

Gently press the giraffe cookie cutter into the top of the cake, so its feet point toward the good side of the cake.

Carefully remove the cookie cutter—the outline should be visible in the frosting. If any frosting pulls away with the cutter, simply pat it back into place with a finger.

Place the orange frosting into a piping bag with the small star tip. Pipe orange spots 1–3 stars big in various places inside the cookie cutter outline.

Remove the tip and empty your piping bag. Clean and dry both thoroughly. Place yellow frosting into the bag with the small star tip (#16) and use it to fill in the remaining spaces with yellow stars. Place the small round compatible tip on your tube of black Decorator's Icing and pipe a small dot for an eye on the giraffe's face (or use tweezers to place a blue or green quin there).

Use your piping bag of green frosting to pipe a shell border around the bottom edge of the cake (where the cake meets the serving plate) and the top edge of the cake—this will conceal any rough patches, and give your cake a more finished look.

SIMPLE STARBURST

This easy-to-decorate birthday cake uses piping gel to transfer the starburst pattern from this book onto your cake.

You Will Need:

- 1 cake recipe, baked as two 8-inch round layers
- 1 recipe Basic Buttercream (page 46)
- 1 filling recipe (or use some of your Basic Buttercream)
- blue, yellow, and red food coloring
- 3 small bowls
- 2 piping bags
- 2 couplers and rings
- large star tip (#21)
- small round tip (#3)
- wax or parchment paper
- clear or white piping gel*

*White piping gel is available in small tubes in the baking section of most grocery stores and can be piped directly from the tube. Clear piping gel comes in a small tub and is available in the cake decorating section of most craft stores. It needs to be put into a piping bag to pipe it.

How to Decorate Simple Starburst Cake

Scoop ½ cup Basic Buttercream into a small bowl and tint it yellow. Place it in a piping bag with a coupler and set it aside.

Scoop ½ cup Basic Buttercream into a small bowl and use yellow and red food coloring to tint it orange. Cover it and set it aside.

Scoop ½ cup Basic Buttercream into a small bowl and tint it blue. Cover it and set it aside.

Put ½ cup white frosting into a piping bag with the large star tip (#21).

Level your cakes, and use the white frosting to pipe a dam around the inside edge of the bottom layer. Fill with your desired filling, and assemble. Crumb-coat and flat-ice the cake with white frosting.

Empty the white frosting out of the piping bag and thoroughly clean and dry the bag, coupler, and tip. Place ½ cup clear piping gel into bag with coupler and small round tip (#3)—if using white piping gel in a tube, you may skip this step and pipe directly from the tube.

Lay a piece of wax or parchment paper over the starburst design in this book, and tape it to the table to hold it in place.

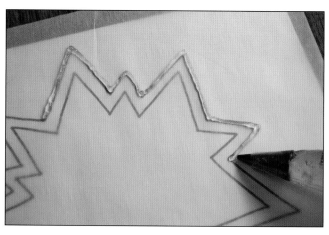

Pipe over all black lines with your piping gel, using the line technique explained on page 24.

Once all the lines are covered with piping gel, unfasten the tape, and carefully pick up your wax/parchment paper. Gently flip the paper over onto the cake, centering it so the image does not hang over any side of the cake.

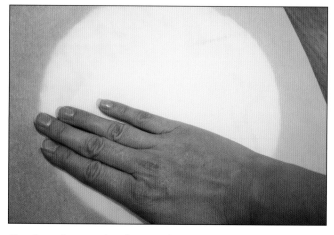

Gently rub your hand over the paper, pressing lightly to transfer the gel onto the cake—don't push too hard, or you'll smear the gel; you only need a small amount of pressure.

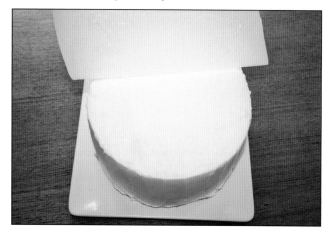

Carefully peel the wax/parchment paper off. The piping gel image should remain on the cake.

Attach the large star tip (#21) to the piping bag of yellow frosting and pipe stars in between the two piping gel lines.

Pipe a border of stars around the bottom edge of the cake (where the cake meets the serving plate).

Empty the other piping bag of piping gel (or white frosting, if you used a tube of white gel) and thoroughly clean and dry the bag and coupler. Remove the star tip from your yellow frosting and clean and dry it as well.

Place your orange frosting into the piping bag, along with a coupler and the large star tip. Pipe orange stars onto one section of the top of the cake, outside the yellow starburst.

Pipe a few scattered stars on the side of the cake, below the orange section.

Move directly across the cake and pipe more orange stars on top of the cake, around the outside of the yellow starburst. Pipe scattered stars on the side of the cake below the orange section.

Empty the piping bag and thoroughly clean and dry the bag, tip, and coupler. Place the blue frosting into the bag with the same coupler and tip.

Pipe blue stars onto the top of the cake in the remaining empty areas outside the yellow starburst. Pipe scattered blue stars on the sides of the cake under the blue sections.

Remove the star tip and replace it with small round tip. Pipe *Happy Birthday* or the inscription of your choice inside the yellow starburst.

PRETEND PIE

Fool your guests by serving them a sweet cherry pie that's actually a Black Forest–style cake in disguise! For double the prank, make up half the cake recipe in a single pie plate, and bake the other half as Chocolate Chip Cookie Surprises (page 67).

You Will Need:

- 1 recipe Chocolate Cake (page 42), baked in two metal pie plates*
- 1 recipe Basic Buttercream (page 46)
- 2 cans of cherry pie filling
- 1 teaspoon cocoa powder

- yellow food coloring
- 1 piping bag
- basketweave tip (#47)
- whipping cream, optional

How to Decorate Pretend Pie

*Note: Do not de-pan these cakes; serve them in their metal pie plates to really make it look like you're serving pie.

If the middles of your cakes have risen a lot higher than the edges, use a serrated knife to level them to the height of the pie plate.

Spread one can of cherry pie filling across each pie, leaving about one-quarter inch bare at the edges, where the cake meets the pan.

Stir cocoa powder and some yellow food coloring into your Basic Buttercream until you reach a light golden brown pastry color. Place the frosting in a piping bag with the basketweave tip—because you want it to look like pastry, you want to keep the serrated edge of the tip pointing down toward the cake at all times, so you are piping smooth lines only for this design.

Pipe a lattice pattern on the top of the cake (see directions on page 30).

Next, pipe the outside crust of the pie. Hold your piping bag at a 45° angle above the outside edge of the cake, slightly overlapping the pie plate. As you squeeze the bag, move it in and out, while also slowly moving it around the outside of the cake, creating a wavy line around the entire outside edge.

Repeat all steps for the second pie.

Serve with whipped cream for a Black Forest–inspired cake taste.

CHOCOLATE CHIP COOKIE SURPRISES

These tricky little treats will leave your guests wondering, where's the cake? For an extra-tricky feast, only make up half of the batter as cupcakes, and use the rest for a Pretend Pie (pg 65).

You Will Need:

- 1 cake recipe, baked as 24 cupcakes
- 1 recipe Basic Buttercream (page 46)
- 1–2 teaspoons cocoa powder
- yellow food coloring

- 1 cup chocolate chips
- biscuit cutter or large flower cookie cutter, optional
- 2 tablespoons cocoa powder, optional

How to Decorate Chocolate Chip Cookie Cupcakes

Stir 1 teaspoon cocoa powder and a small amount of yellow food coloring into frosting, adjusting amounts until you end up with a cookie-color frosting. Flat-ice a cupcake.

Sprinkle chocolate chips on top.

How to Make Bite Marks

Sit a biscuit cutter or large flower cookie cutter on top of an un-frosted cupcake and frost up to the side of the cutter.

Remove the cookie cutter, leaving curved "bite marks." (You may need to adjust the frosting with a toothpick or skewer to make it look just right.)

If using chocolate cupcakes, you have the option of just not frosting a small area of the cupcake and leaving the plain cupcake as the "bite." Otherwise, add 2 tablespoons cocoa powder to remaining frosting and stir well. Use this chocolate frosting to fill in the empty space, creating your "bite mark."

DELECTABLE DONUT

This yummy treat is so simple to make, the hardest part will be finding a big enough cup of coffee to go with it.

You Will Need:

- 1 cake recipe, baked in a Bundt pan
- ½ recipe white chocolate ganache variation (2 ounces cream: 3½ ounces white chocolate—see instructions on page 44)
- red liquid food coloring
- ½ cup jelly beans
- sharp knife
- cutting board

How to Decorate Delectable Donut Cake

De-pan your cake. Level the cake and flip it onto a serving plate, so the top of the cake is the part that was cooked in the pan.

Make the ganache. When it is time to stir it, add 2–3 drops of red food coloring. Let the ganache sit for another 10–20 minutes or until it has reached the consistency of soft margarine.

While waiting, slice the jelly beans lengthwise with a sharp knife—be careful! They slide when cutting (*younger bakers should ask for help from an adult*). The best method I have found is to stick the point of the knife in first, then slice.

Once you think the ganache has reached the consistency of soft margarine, spread one spoonful of it on top of the cake. If the ganache slides off the cake, it is not set enough. Simply wipe up any mess, and let your ganache sit longer. Ganache that is the right consistency will spread slightly, but remain on top of the cake.

Once the ganache is ready, spoon it over the cake.

Place the jelly bean halves cut-side down on ganache.

BEAUTIFUL BOUQUET

What's better than a bouquet of flowers? A bouquet made out of cupcakes!

You Will Need:

- 1 cake recipe, baked as 12 cupcakes + 1 loaf cake
- 1 recipe Basic Buttercream—*stiff* consistency (page 46)
- red, blue, and yellow food coloring
- 2 tablespoons water
- 4 small bowls
- 4 piping bags
- 1 coupler and ring

- large round tip (#12)
- cupcake-filling tip (#230)
- petal tip (#103)
- small flower tip (#225)
- 1 strawberry Fruit by the Foot
- 1 package green shoelace candy
- 5 spearmint leaf candies
- sharp knife

How to Decorate Vase

Place the loaf cake either on a small plate, or on a 12 x 15-inch cake board or covered cookie sheet.

Scoop 1½ cups Basic Buttercream into a small bowl. Use red food coloring to tint it dark pink. Place the frosting in a piping bag with a coupler and the large round tip (#12).

Add water 1 tablespoon at a time to remaining undyed frosting, until thin consistency is reached.

Flat-ice the loaf cake with uncolored (white) frosting. While the frosting is still wet, place a strip of strawberry Fruit by the Foot across the width of the cake, about a third of the way down the length. Cut off any excess with a sharp knife.

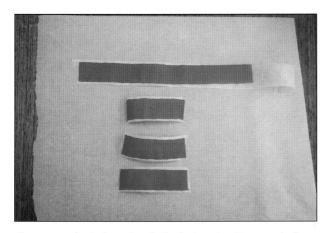

Cut one 8-inch length of Fruit by the Foot and three 3-inch lengths.

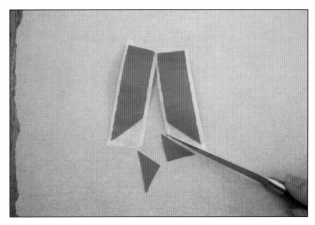

Cut one end of two of the 3-inch lengths in a diagonal line—these will be the fancy ends of the bow ribbon.

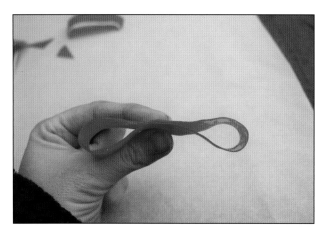

Bend the two ends of the 8-inch length in toward the center, so they meet in the middle.

Wrap the remaining 3-inch length of Fruit by the Foot around the center of the folded 8-inch length.

Squeeze a dot of pink frosting from your piping bag onto the Fruit by the Foot on the loaf cake. Place the two cut 3-inch lengths on the frosting, letting the diagonal ends hang below the Fruit by the Foot on the cake.

Use a dot of pink frosting to attach it to the Fruit by the Foot on the loaf cake, directly on top of the tops of the 2-inch lengths.

Set vase cake aside.

Scoop 1 cup Basic Buttercream into a small bowl and tint it pale green with yellow and blue food coloring. Use this to flat-ice your cupcakes.

Roses:

Follow the directions for piping roses found on page 31 and pipe a rose directly onto a cupcake. Continue piping petals until the entire cupcake is covered.

Do this on four cupcakes.

Hydrangea:

Scoop 1 cup Basic Buttercream into a small bowl and use blue and red food coloring to tint the frosting a light purply-blue. Place the frosting in a piping bag with the small flower tip (#225).

See piping tips for Simple Flowers on page 26, but leave the centers empty. Cover the entire top of the cupcake with simple flowers.

Do this on four cupcakes.

Daisies:

Scoop 1 cup undyed (white) frosting into a piping bag with the cupcake-filling tip (#230). Hold your bag at a 90° angle at the outside edge of the cupcake, facing toward the center of the cupcake.

Squeeze the bag gently, while pulling your hand toward the center of the cupcake. Release pressure at center of the cupcake, and remove the bag.

Move over about the width of your piping tip and again pipe a line from the outside edge of the cupcake to the center.

Continue repeating until you have come around to your first line.

Pipe more petals on top of the empty spaces.

Continue until all the empty spaces have been filled in.

Do this for four cupcakes.

Scoop ½ cup undyed frosting into a small bowl and tint it bright yellow. Place it in a piping bag with the large round tip (#12)—make sure you have thoroughly cleaned and dried it after piping your roses.

Pipe a large dot in the center of each daisy.

How to Assemble the Beautiful Bouquet

If you used a small plate for your vase cake, you must assemble your bouquet where you want to display it. Otherwise you can assemble the bouquet on your 12 x 15-inch cake board or cookie sheet.

Cut twelve 8-inch lengths of green shoelace candy. Stick one end of each candy into the "top" of the vase—not the top of the cake where the ribbon is, but where the flowers would go if it was a real vase.

Spread the other ends of the shoelace candy across the top of the cake board/cookie sheet/display area. Arrange your flower cupcakes on top of the spread-out ends of the shoelace candies.

Hold a spearmint leaf on its side and use a sharp knife to slice it in half. Do this for all five leaves. Arrange the ten leaf-halves, cut-side down, on top of the upper ends of the green shoelace candies.

CUTIE BUG CAKE

Normally you wouldn't want bugs crawling all over your cake, but you'll make an exception when you see how cute these ones are.

You Will Need:

- 1 cake recipe, baked in two 8-inch rounds
- 1 recipe Basic Buttercream (page 46)
- yellow and blue food coloring
- filling of your choice (or use some of your green frosting)
- 2 small bowls
- 1 tube red Decorator's Icing
- 1 tube black Decorator's Icing
- 3 piping bags
- 3 couplers and rings

- large round tip (#12)
- medium round tip (#5)
- small round tip (#3)
- cupcake-filling tip (#230)
- small round tip (#3) compatible with Decorator's Icing
- large round tip (#12) compatible with Decorator's Icing
- toothpick or skewer

How to Decorate Cutie Bug Cake

Place 1 cup of uncolored (white) Basic Buttercream in a piping bag with your cupcake-filling tip (#230). Set it aside.

Scoop 1 cup Basic Buttercream into a small bowl and tint it yellow. Place it in a piping bag with a coupler and ring. Set it aside.

Tint the remaining Basic Buttercream pale green. Place 1 cup green frosting into a piping bag with a coupler and large round (#12) tip. Use it to pipe a dam around the bottom layer of cake.

Fill and assemble the cake. Use pale green frosting to crumb-coat, then flat-ice the cake.

Pick the best side of your cake (the one that looks the most level, and has the smoothest frosting). This will be the front of your cake. Starting at the back of the cake, use your piping bag of green frosting to pipe 6 large dots around the bottom edge of the cake (where the cake meets the plate). Leave a space slightly larger than one dot, then pipe six more dots around the base of the cake. Continue piping dots, leaving a space after every sixth dot, until you have gone around the entire base of the cake.

Remove the tip, wash and thoroughly dry it.

Get your piping bag of white frosting with the cupcake-filling tip (#230). Hold it just above the top of the cake at a 90° angle, about two inches from the cake's center (you can mark the center with a toothpick to make this easier). Pipe a daisy onto the center of the top of the cake (see directions in Beautiful Bouquet on page 73).

Squeeze the remaining frosting out into a small bowl. Remove the tip. Insert a coupler and refill the bag with white frosting.

Place your large round tip (#12) on the piping bag full of yellow frosting. Use it to pipe a large dot on the center of your daisy.

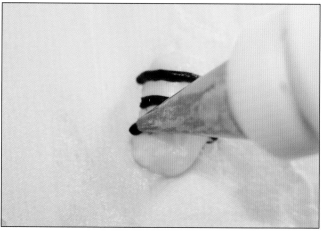

Next, hold your yellow piping bag at a 45° angle, to one side of the daisy. Squeeze out the frosting, and slowly move the bag forward, until you have an elongated dot about 1 inch long. Pipe two to three more of these on various locations on the cake, leaving lots of space between them.

Attach your small round compatible tip (#3) to the black Decorator's Icing. Pipe 3 stripes across each yellow oblong. Use a toothpick, if necessary, to help anchor the ends of the stripes.

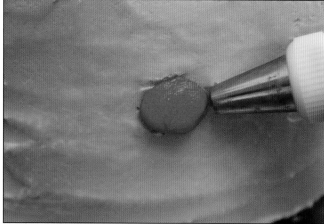

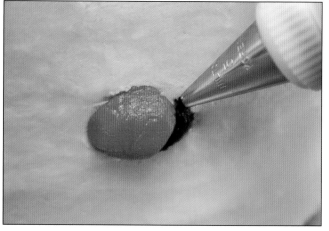

Put your large round compatible tip on the tube of red Decorator's Icing (if using the same tip as before, make sure to thoroughly clean and dry it first). Use the same technique that you did with the yellow frosting to make two or three oversize dots (about half an inch long) on the cake.

Using your black Decorator's Icing with the medium round tip, pipe a large dot at one end of the red dot (ladybug's head).

Next, pipe a straight line from the head all the way across the middle of the back, and pipe two to three small dots on each side of the line. Use a toothpick to help anchor or flatten the frosting, as necessary.

Attach the medium round tip (#5) to the piping bag of white frosting (if you're using the same tip you used for the black frosting, be sure to thoroughly clean and dry it before attaching). Pipe a small figure eight on the back of each bee.

Using the black Decorator's Icing, pipe meandering dotted lines from the back of each bug to either the large daisy, or one of the empty spaces on the bottom border.

Next, go down to the bottom border and pipe daisies in the empty spaces with your medium round tip (#5), using the same technique as you used for the large daisy at the center of the cake.

Attach your small round tip (#3) to your piping bag full of yellow frosting and pipe small dots in the center of each daisy.

FABULOUS FROGS

These adorable cupcakes are simple to make and sure to put a smile on your face.

You Will Need:

- 1 cake recipe, baked as 24 cupcakes
- 1 frosting recipe
- green food coloring
- 48 white chocolate melting wafers

- 48 brown M&M's Minis
- 24 red juicy gel candies
- sharp knife
- cutting board

How to Decorate Fabulous Frogs:

Tint your frosting green and flat-ice the cupcakes.

Place two white chocolate melting wafers on the top of each cupcake at one end.

Spread a small amount of frosting on the back of each M&M's Mini and attach each one to the center of one of the white chocolate melting wafers.

Use a sharp knife to cut the "rind" off of all the juicy gel candies.

Discard the rind, and place the center part of each juicy gel candy on top of a cupcake, under the melting wafer eyes.

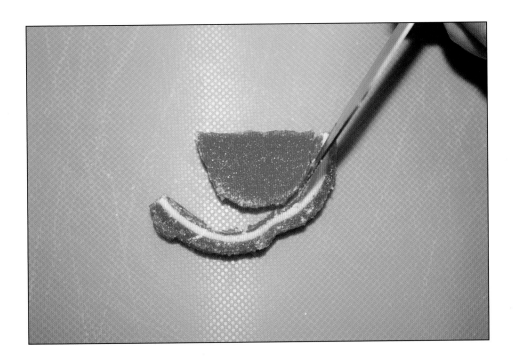

SMILING SNOWMAN

This happy little guy is easy to make and great for winter parties. The only problem? He's so cute, your guests won't want to eat him!

You Will Need:

- 1 cake recipe, baked in two 8-inch round pans
- 1 filling recipe, or use your white frosting
- 1 recipe Basic Buttercream (page 46)
- 1 piping bag
- large round piping tip (#12)
- 7 dark chocolate melting wafers
- 1 orange Tootsie Roll candy
- 1 roll Berry Tie-Dye Fruit by the Foot

How to Decorate Smiling Snowman Cake

Place 1 cup white (uncolored) Basic Buttercream into a piping bag with the large round tip (#12).

Level, fill, and assemble your two 8-inch layers, using your piping bag of white frosting to pipe a dam.

Crumb-coat and flat-ice your cake with white frosting.

Place two melting wafer eyes near the center of the cake. Leave a space for the nose to go, and arrange the rest of your melting wafers below as a smile.

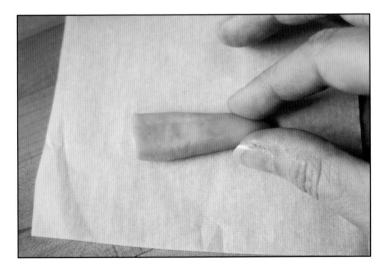

Using your hands, pinch one end of the orange Tootsie Roll, forming it into a point, then flatten the candy against the table with your hand.

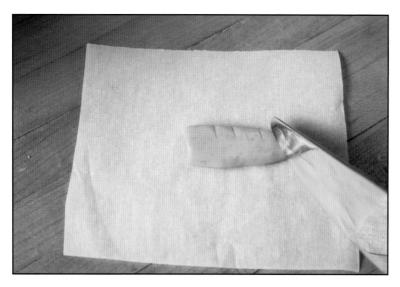

Use a knife to lightly score one side of the now-carrot-shaped roll. Place the carrot nose on the cake between the eyes and mouth.

Roll out your Fruit by the Foot onto a piece of wax or parchment paper, in the rough shape of a hat, overlapping the edges of each piece.

Sit your 8-inch cake pan on top to measure, and trim them to the size of your cake.

Carefully move the Fruit by the Foot hat over onto the cake.

Use your piping bag of white frosting to pipe trim around the bottom of the hat by holding the piping bag at a 45° angle and squeezing. Release pressure slightly, move your hand ¼ inch along the cake, and increase pressure. Continue squeezing, releasing, and moving until trim is complete.

Pipe a large dot at the top of the hat.

Pipe a dot border around the bottom edge of the cake to hide the messy edge where the cake meets the plate.

S'MORES CAMPING CAKE

Nothing says camping like gooey, chocolaty s'mores, a tent, and a good old-fashioned campfire.

You Will Need:

- 1 recipe Chocolate Cake (page 42), baked in two 8-inch round pans
- 1 recipe Gooey Marshmallow Filling (page 45)
- 1 recipe Basic Buttercream (page 46)
- medium bowl
- 2 tablespoons cocoa powder
- 1 box chocolate-covered finger cookies
- 1 piece of string or twine
- green food coloring

- 2 piping bags
- grass/hair tip (#233)
- large round tip (#12)
- 2 graham crackers
- 1 large marshmallow
- 1 roll Fruit by the Foot (or similar product), green
- 6 chocolate pebbles
- two 2-inch pieces of Life Saver Fire (see directions on page 38)

How to Decorate S'mores Camping Cake

Scoop half of the frosting into a bowl and stir in cocoa powder. Place ½ cup of chocolate frosting into a piping bag with your large round tip (#12). Pipe a dam on the bottom layer cake.

Fill the cake with Gooey Marshmallow Filling and assemble.

Crumb-coat and flat-ice the cake with the remaining chocolate frosting—don't worry about making the frosting too perfect, since it will all be covered.

Measure one of your chocolate finger cookies against the side of the cake, and cut it so it stands about one-quarter inch taller than the cake. Cut all of your finger cookies to this length.

Stand the chocolate finger cookies around outside of cake, gently pushing them into the chocolate frosting to stay.

Loop the string around cake and tie in a bow *(remember to remove the string before cutting and serving).*

Tint the remaining uncolored frosting green. Place the green frosting and the grass/hair tip (#233) into another piping bag. Pipe grass over the top of cake, leaving one small bare patch of chocolate frosting at the front right (this will be your fire pit). Place a ring of chocolate pebbles around the outside of the chocolate patch.

Cut the marshmallow in half (I find scissors work best for this), and sit half of it on a 3-inch long strip of green Fruit by the Foot, forming a sleeping bag and pillow.

Carefully tent the two graham crackers on either side of the sleeping bag, and pipe a small line of chocolate frosting along the top edge to seal the pieces together. Sit these on the grass, back and to the left of the fire pit, leaving space around them on all sides. Cut a few of your leftover pieces of finger cookies into small lengths and place them in the fire pit as logs.

Shortly before serving, gently sit fire pieces inside the fire pit, pressing the yellow ends carefully into the cake—you don't want to do this too early, or the candy will absorb moisture from the cake and frosting and start to melt.

UNDERWATER WONDERLAND

Fabulous for mermaid-lovers and aspiring marine biologists, one of the greatest things about this cake is that your flat-icing doesn't have to be perfect because the wavy water hides all your spatula marks.

You Will Need:

- 1 cake recipe, baked as two 8-inch round layers
- 1 recipe Basic Buttercream (page 46)
- filling of your choice (or use some of your blue frosting)
- blue and red liquid food coloring
- 2 Color by the Foot Fruit by the Foot rolls
- sharp knife
- cutting board
- ¼ cup edible sand (see directions on page 38)
- ½ cup ocean gummies/Swedish Fish
- 4 large yellow star quins
- 3 piping bags
- large round tip (#12) or large star tip (#21)
- small round tip (#3)
- medium round tip (#5)

How to Decorate Underwater Wonderland Cake

Scoop ¼ cup Basic Buttercream into one of the piping bags along with the medium round tip (#5). Set it aside.

Use the blue liquid food coloring to tint the remaining frosting blue. Scoop ½ cup blue frosting into a piping bag with either your large round tip (#12) or your large star tip (#21).

Level your cakes, and use the blue frosting to pipe a dam around the bottom layer. Fill it with your desired filling. Assemble the cake, then crumb-coat it and flat-ice it with blue frosting—don't worry about getting your frosting too perfect—in fact, the more sideways spatula lines, the better.

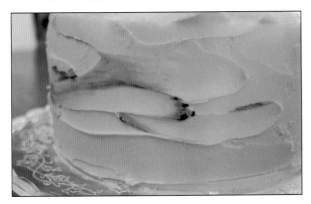

Carefully place one drop of blue food coloring on your frosting spatula and use it to smooth over the cake in a side-to-side motion, creating waves. Each time your spatula runs out of color, drip another drop on, and repeat until the cake is covered with "waves."

Open the Fruit by the Foot and use your sharp knife to cut off the green section. Slice the green candy into wavy lines.

Cut out a length of yellow Fruit by the Foot. Slice it width-wise into approximately $1/16$-inch strips (about the width of a toothpick).

Place the green candy slices in groups of two and three, up the outside edges of the cake, starting at the bottom.

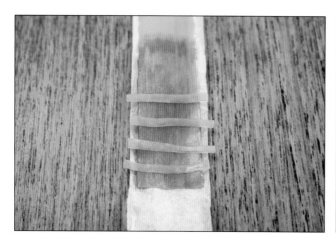

Cut out a length of orange Fruit by the Foot. Moisten the orange candy with a drop of water—don't use too much, you just want to get the candy sticky, not melt it—and lay the yellow strips across the width of the orange candy.

Roll the strip lengthwise, yellow stripes out.

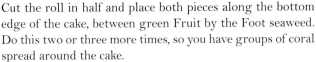

Cut the roll in half and place both pieces along the bottom edge of the cake, between green Fruit by the Foot seaweed. Do this two or three more times, so you have groups of coral spread around the cake.

Spoon your edible sand mixture along the bottom edge of the cake.

Place the large yellow star quins in various places around the bottom edge of the cake, as starfish.

Place gummy seashells, if you have them, along the bottom edge of the cake.

Gently press gummy fish into the sides of the cake at different heights—it will look best if you try to spread out the different colors.

Use your bag of white Buttercream to pipe three small dots above each fish's mouth, as bubbles.

Stir some red food coloring into remaining blue frosting to create a reddish-purple. Place this frosting in a piping bag with your small round tip (#3). Pipe *Happy Birthday* (or the inscription of your choice) on the top of the cake.

Arrange a yellow star quin, gummy fish, and shells around the lettering on top of the cake.

SUPERHERO CUPCAKES

It's a bird, it's a plane, it's super cupcakes! The best part about these treats is that you can make them to match the birthday kid's favorite hero, or personalize them, and turn each of your guests into their own comic character.

You Will Need:

- 1 cake recipe, baked as 24 cupcakes
- 1 recipe Basic Buttercream frosting (page 46)
- 3 medium bowls
- yellow and red food coloring
- 1–2 tablespoons cocoa powder
- 1 empty cupcake liner
- sharp knife
- 2–3 piping bags or small plastic bags

- grass/hair tip (#233)
- 2–3 Fruit by the Foot rolls (Color by the Foot and Strawberry)
- 48 large candy eyeballs
- 1 tube red Decorator's Icing
- 1 tube black Decorator's Icing
- medium round tip (#5) compatible with Decorator's tube

How to Decorate Superhero Cupcakes

Scoop 1 cup Basic Buttercream into a medium bowl. Using a small amount of red food coloring, tint the frosting light pink (for a more realistic skin tone, try adding a drop of yellow). Set it aside.

Scoop 1 cup frosting into another medium bowl. Using yellow food coloring and ½ teaspoon cocoa powder, tint the frosting pale beige or golden brown.

Scoop 1 cup buttercream frosting into your third medium bowl. Add 1 tablespoon cocoa powder (if your frosting becomes too thick, add ¼ teaspoon water).

Use the pink, beige, and brown frosting to flat-ice eight cupcakes each.

Using your empty cupcake liner as a guide, trim strips of Fruit by the Foot with sharp knife to match the size of the cupcake top.

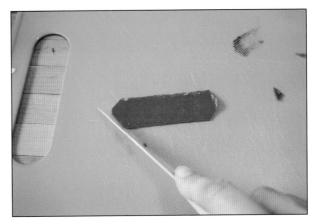

Trim the corners off the Fruit by the Foot strip.

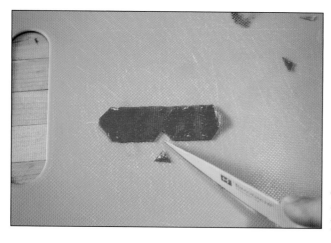

Cut a small triangle out of the bottom middle of the Fruit by the Foot strip. Cut a larger triangle out of the top middle of the Fruit by the Foot strip.

Lay the Fruit by the Foot mask across the top of cupcake, just above center.

Sit two candy eyeballs on top of Fruit by the Foot (if the eyeballs won't stick, use a small dab of frosting on the back of them as glue).

Attach your medium round compatible tip (#5) to your Decorator's Icing and pipe smiles below the masks.

Tint the remaining white frosting yellow, and use yellow, brown, and black frosting to pipe hair according to the instructions below.

Piping Short Hair

Use your grass/hair tip (#233) attached to a piping bag, small plastic bag, or tube of Decorator's Icing. Start at one side of the cupcake, just above the mask. Hold your bag/tube at a 90° angle just above the cupcake.

Give the bag a quick squeeze, release pressure, and pull the bag away. Move your bag over to an empty space and repeat, working your way across the cupcake's head.

Piping Long Hair

Use your grass/hair tip (#233) attached to a piping bag, small plastic bag, or tube of Decorator's Icing. Hold your bag/tube at a 90° angle, just above the center of the mask. In one fluid motion, squeeze the bag and move your hand across the top of the cupcake, over the edge of the mask, down to the "chin." Release, and remove the bag. Repeat on the other side of the cupcake.

Piping Curly Hair

Use your medium round tip (#5) attached to a piping bag, small plastic bag, or tube of Decorator's Icing. Start at one side of the cupcake, just above the mask. Hold your bag at a 90° angle, just above the cupcake. In one fluid motion, squeeze the bag and move your hand in small circles, working your way across the cupcake. Release and remove the bag when finished.

OUT OF THIS WORLD SPACE CAKE

Great for sci-fi fans and budding astronauts, your guests will think this space cake is out of this world.

You Will Need:

- 1 cake recipe, baked as two 8-inch rounds
- 1 recipe Basic Buttercream (page 46)
- red, yellow, blue, and green liquid food coloring
- black gel coloring
- 1 recipe filling (or use some of your gray frosting)
- 1–2 tablespoons cocoa powder
- 6 small bowls
- 5 small plastic bags
- scissors
- 2 piping bags
- large star tip (#21)
- large round tip (#12)
- 10 large yellow star quins
- 20 small yellow star quins
- 10 yellow and white sequins (round quins)

How to Decorate Out of this World Space Cake

Scoop 2 tablespoons Basic Buttercream into a small bowl and tint it dark pink. Cover it and set it aside.

Scoop 2 tablespoons Basic Buttercream into a small bowl and use red and yellow food coloring to tint it orange. Cover it and set it aside.

Scoop 2 tablespoons Basic Buttercream into a small bowl and tint it a medium blue (earth-colored). Place the blue frosting in the corner of a plastic bag. Squeeze out all air, seal it closed, and set it aside.

Scoop 2 tablespoons Basic Buttercream into a small bowl and tint it green. Place the green frosting in the corner of a plastic bag. Squeeze out all air, seal it closed, and set it aside.

Scoop 2 tablespoons Basic Buttercream into a small bowl and use red and blue food coloring to tint it purple. Place the purple frosting in the corner of a plastic bag. Squeeze out all air, seal it closed, and set it aside.

Scoop 1 cup Basic Buttercream into a small bowl and tint it yellow. Place it in a piping bag along with your large star tip (#21) and set it aside.

Stir 1 tablespoon cocoa powder and black food coloring into the remaining uncolored frosting, until it becomes dark gray (for a richer gray, add a drop or two of red and green liquid color). Let the frosting sit, covered, for about ten minutes so the colors can fully develop. If the resulting color is too purple, stir in a drop of green; if it is too green, stir in a drop of red.

Place 1 cup of gray frosting into a piping bag with the large round tip (#12).

Level your cake. Use the gray frosting to pipe a dam. Fill with your desired filling. Assemble the cake, and use the gray frosting to crumb-coat and flat-ice it.

Arrange the large and small star quins and the sequins randomly around the cake, leaving space for planets (if you're not sure how much space to leave, you can save this step for the end).

Scoop the orange frosting into the corner of a bag, trying to keep it to one side of the bag.

Scoop the dark pink frosting into the other side of the same corner of the bag.

Squeeze out all air and seal the bag shut. Twist the bag just above the frosting, to force frosting down into the corner. Snip off the corner of the bag, about one-quarter inch in.

Hold the bag at a 90° angle and pipe a ½-inch-diameter circle on the cake. Release pressure and pull the bag away. While the frosting is still wet, carefully use your finger to swirl the colors together, and pat it flat.

Repeat on two or three other locations on the cake, including one on the top.

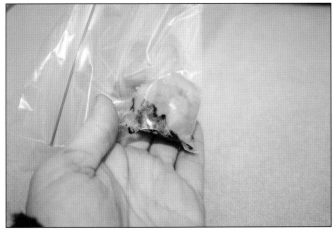

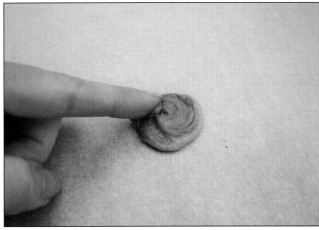

Open the bag with the blue frosting, and drip one to two drops of green liquid food coloring down the side. Squeeze out all air and seal the bag closed. Twist the bag just above the frosting, forcing it down into the corner. Snip about ¼ inch off corner with scissors.

Find an empty space on the cake. Hold the bag at a 90° angle and pipe a ½-inch-diameter dot. Release pressure and pull the bag away. Use a finger to swirl the green and blue together, if necessary. Repeat on two or three other locations on the cake, including the top.

Take your bag of green frosting and twist it just above the frosting, pushing it down toward the corner. Snip ¼ inch off the corner. Find an empty spot on the cake and, pipe a ¾-inch-diameter dot on the cake. Do this on several other locations on the cake, including the top.

Take your bag of purple frosting and twist it so the frosting is forced into the corner of the bag. Snip ⅛-inch off corner—*note: this is smaller than the other corners cut so far*. Hold your bag at a 90° angle, just above and to the side of one of the green dots. Pipe a line across the center of the green circle, ending on the gray frosting beside it, creating the appearance of rings around your green planet.

If your line isn't thick enough, pipe a second purple line beside the first, and pat into place once frosting has formed a crust (about 5–10 minutes later).

Repeat this for the other green circles.

Take your piping bag of yellow frosting and pipe a border of stars across the bottom edge of the cake, to hide the messy edge where the cake meets the plate.

STUNNING SNOWFLAKES

These beauties are simple to make and perfect for a winter or winter-themed party. I have included eight snowflake patterns for you to copy (make three of each design for 24 cupcakes), or you can create your own designs for 24 unique snowflakes.

You Will Need:

- 1 cake recipe, baked as 24 cupcakes
- 1 recipe Basic Buttercream frosting (page 46)
- blue and yellow food coloring
- piping bag
- small round tip (#3)
- ¼ cup silver dragées
- tweezers

How to Decorate Stunning Snowflake Cupcakes

Place 1 cup of uncolored frosting into your piping bag with your small round tip (#3).

Use two to three drops of blue coloring and one drop of yellow to tint the remaining frosting pale turquoise. Use the pale turquoise frosting to flat-ice the cupcakes.

Use your bag of white frosting to pipe snowflakes on top of the cupcakes.

To help make your snowflakes come out even, start by marking the center of your cupcake with a dot of frosting—if you're really worried about making your lines perfect, use a toothpick or skewer to lightly trace your snowflake design onto the top of the cupcake, then simply pipe over the lines with frosting.

Use the straight line technique (page 24) to pipe a line from one side of the cupcake to the other, going through the center. Your cupcake should now be divided into two sides by a white line.

Start one-third of the way around one side and draw another straight line all the way across the cupcake, again going through the center.

Start halfway between your last line and the end of the first line, and pipe another straight line across the cupcake, again going through the center. Your cupcake should now have six equal sections on top. Every new line you draw after this should be repeated five more times (once for each of the main six lines).

If this all sounds too scary or complicated, simply use the reverse image transfer technique described on page 34 with a tube of white piping gel to transfer the snowflake designs from this book directly onto your cupcakes (since snowflakes are symmetrical, there's no need to reverse the image).

Use tweezers to place silver dragées on the center and each point of the snowflake.

COLORFUL CAKES

With these designs, it's the cake that's the star of the show, while the frosting is just, well, the frosting on top.

From colorful cupcakes to a quin-studded confetti treat, to a bright wannabe watermelon, these cakes are sure to delight any color-loving birthday kid or kid at heart.

Doubtful about dark colors? Tone it down a notch by simply using less food coloring to get softer, more pastel shades for your cake and frosting.

RAINBOW PERFECTION

These colorful beauties will leave your guests oohing and aahing as they peel away the wrapper and realize it's the cake, not the cover, that's rainbow-striped.

You Will Need:

- 1 recipe pound cake, made up with egg whites only (or 1 box white cake mix + 1 teaspoon clear vanilla)—see baking directions below
- blue, red, and yellow food coloring
- 18 white cupcake liners
- 6 small bowls

- 1 recipe Basic Buttercream (*stiff consistency*) (page 46)
- piping bag
- extra-large star tip (#1M)
- ½ cup rainbow sprinkles
- ½ cup rainbow sequins/round quins

How to Dye Your Batter for Rainbow Perfection Cupcakes

Scoop ⅓ cup of batter into one of your bowls. Tint it purple using red and blue food coloring.

Colors fade during baking, so be sure to tint your batter darker than you think you need (start with about a ½ teaspoon of the gel color). Make sure you stir thoroughly, scraping the sides of the bowl, to fully mix the color into the batter.

Scoop ½ cup of uncolored batter into another bowl. Color it blue.

Scoop about ⅔ cup of uncolored batter into another bowl. Use blue and yellow food coloring to tint it green.

Scoop about ¾ cup of uncolored batter into another bowl. Color it yellow.

Scoop about 1 cup of uncolored batter into another bowl. Color it orange using red and yellow food coloring.

Scoop about 1¼ cups of uncolored batter into the last bowl. Color it dark pink/red.

If you have any batter left over, share it out equally between the bowls. (Remember, you want to have the most red batter, then orange, then yellow, etc. ending with the least amount of purple batter—this is because cupcakes are smaller at the base than at the top.) You will need to add extra food coloring if you add more batter.

You should now have six different colors of batter, one in each bowl: purple, blue, green, yellow, orange, and red.

How to Bake Rainbow Perfection Cupcakes

This next part is simple, but time-consuming. Make sure to leave yourself sufficient time: about 45 minutes to one hour.

Line your cupcake pans with the white liners.

Place a teaspoon of purple batter in the bottom of each liner, spreading it around so it covers the whole bottom.

Gently place a teaspoon of blue batter directly on top of the purple, starting around the outside edges, and working your way in to the center (this is to make sure the edges show the rainbow stripes when finished). You will need to work carefully, so you don't mix the two colors together—you want the cupcakes to end up layered, not swirled.

Continue the process with the green, yellow, orange, and red batters. Bake at 350°F for 15–25 minutes (they take longer than other cupcakes because they're bigger).

Cool completely before frosting.

How to Decorate Rainbow Perfection Cupcakes

Place white (uncolored) Basic Buttercream into a piping bag with the extra-large star tip (1M). Pipe swirls on top of the cupcakes (see instructions in Classic Cupcakes, page 53).

Mix sprinkles and quins together in a small bowl. Spoon them onto the frosting while it is still wet.

TERRIFIC TIE-DYE CUPCAKES

These colorful cupcakes are the perfect treat for a Groovy Sixties theme party or a birthday kid who loves colors.

You Will Need:

- 1 recipe pound cake, made up with egg whites only or 1 box white cake mix + 1 teaspoon clear vanilla—see baking directions below
- green, blue, purple, red, orange, and yellow gel food coloring
- 24 white cupcake liners
- 6 small to medium bowls
- 1 recipe Basic Buttercream *(stiff consistency)* (page 46)
- disposable piping bag or plastic bag (the bag-streaking effect will permanently dye a reusable piping bag)
- extra-large star tip (#1M)
- toothpicks

How to Bake Tie-Dye Cupcakes

Divide the uncooked cake batter in two. Leave one half in the mixing bowl (it will stay white). Separate the remaining batter into your six bowls and dye one each color with your food coloring.* Remember colors fade during baking, so be sure to tint the batter a bit darker than you want your final shade to be. Put your white liners in your cupcake pan.

Dab in one teaspoon of colored batter, followed by one teaspoon of white (you want your final cupcake to be one-third to one-half white). Put the different colors of batter in randomly—you want the cupcakes to all turn out different.

Once your cupcake liner is two-thirds full, use a toothpick or skewer to gently swirl the batter together—be careful not to overmix or you'll end up with brownish-gray cupcakes. Bake according to cupcake directions.

*Really, the colors are up to you. If you use fewer colors for your cupcakes, use those same colors to line your piping bag for decorating.

How to Decorate Terrific Tie-Dye Cupcakes
Place your extra-large star tip (#1M) into your piping bag.

Before you put in any frosting, coat a toothpick in red gel food coloring and use it to draw a line up the inside of the piping bag, from the piping tip, halfway up to the mouth of the bag.

Coat a toothpick in orange gel food coloring, and draw another line about a sixth of the way around the piping bag, again from the tip halfway up to the mouth of the bag. If you don't have orange gel food coloring, scoop some yellow gel food coloring and some red gel food coloring into a small bowl and mix them together with a toothpick until they make orange. Use this mixture to line your bag.

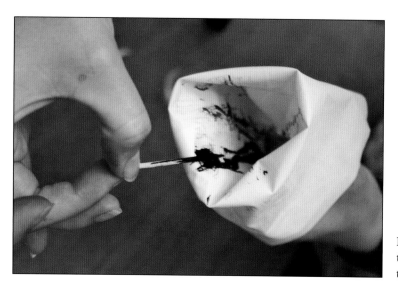

Repeat with the other four colors, moving along the bag (the purple should end up the closest color to the red).

Carefully scoop your frosting into the piping bag, trying to not scrape the sides of the bag. Pipe swirls on top of each cupcake according to the instructions in Classic Cupcakes (page 53). When you refill your bag with more frosting, re-streak the sides with more food coloring.

For more pastel colors, divide your frosting in half. Leave one half white, and separate the other half into six bowls. Tint the six bowls of frosting pastel shades of pink, orange, yellow, green, blue, and mauve. Use a spatula to scrape a tablespoon of pink frosting up the side of the piping bag. Turn your bag and use your spatula to spread a streak of orange frosting up the bag. Continue streaking each of the frosting colors up the side of the bag. Fill the bag with white frosting and pipe swirls on top of each cupcake.

CONFETTI CONFECTION

This beautiful cake is designed to look like a cascade of confetti—inside and out.

You Will Need:
- 1 recipe vanilla Pound Cake (page 41), or vanilla cake mix—baking directions are below
- two 8-inch round layer pans, greased and floured
- 1 small bowl
- 1 recipe Basic Buttercream (page 46)
- ¼ cup rainbow sequins/round quins
- 1 jar rainbow round sprinkles
- piping bag or large plastic bag

How to Bake Confetti Confection Cake
Preheat oven to 350°F.

Scoop 1 cup cake batter into a small bowl. Stir in 5 teaspoons rainbow sequins. Spread the batter in one of the 8-inch round layer pans.

Scoop another 1 cup of cake batter into the small bowl. Stir in 3 teaspoons of rainbow sequins. Carefully spread this batter on top of the other batter in the layer pan. Try not to overmix; you want the batters to form a layered effect. Set the pan aside.

Scoop another 1 cup of batter into the small bowl. Stir in 1 teaspoon rainbow sequins. Spread this in the bottom of your empty layer pan. Carefully spread the remaining cake batter on top, again, trying not mix the two layers together.

Bake both 8-inch layers for 20–30 minutes.

Completely cool cakes before assembling and decorating.

How to Assemble and Decorate Confetti Confection Cake

Level both cakes.

Take the cake with the fewest quins and place it upside down (cut-side down) on your serving plate—this should be the side with no quins in it.

Place ½ cup Basic Buttercream into a piping bag or plastic bag with the end snipped off, and pipe a dam around the outside edge of the cake. Spread vanilla frosting inside the dam, and sprinkle it with 1 teaspoon rainbow sequins.

Place the second layer cut-side down on top of the filling. Crumb-coat and flat-ice the cake with white frosting.

Working quickly, while the frosting is still wet, pour 1 teaspoon round sprinkles into your hand. Hold your hand beside the top edge of the cake, and gently tip the sprinkles onto the edge of the cake, allowing some to trickle down the side of the cake.Repeat until the entire top edge of the cake is covered in round sprinkles.

Where necessary, add individual sprinkles on the sides of the cake, to make it look like confetti is cascading down. Allow fallen sprinkles to pool around the bottom edge of the cake.

Pour 2 tablespoons round sprinkles onto the center of the top of the cake. Use a clean spatula to spread them around the cake.

Add more sprinkles as necessary, and continue spreading until the top of the cake is entirely covered in sprinkles.

WONDERFUL WATERMELON

This tasty fruit is everybody's warm weather favorite. Perfect for summer birthdays or picnic parties, you can't go wrong with watermelon.

You Will Need:
- 1 recipe Pound Cake (page 41) (see baking directions below)
- small metal mixing bowl
- rubber spatula
- red food coloring
- 1 cup jumbo chocolate chips, or chocolate rosettes, halved
- 1 recipe Basic Buttercream (page 46)
- green and yellow liquid food coloring

How to Bake Wonderful Watermelon
Preheat oven to 350°F. Grease and flour your small metal mixing bowl. Scoop 1½ cups pound cake batter into the greased bowl.

Use red food coloring to tint the remaining cake batter a deep pink/red. Stir in the chocolate chip/rosette halves.

Use your rubber spatula to push the uncolored cake batter up the sides of the small metal mixing bowl. The batter is thick, and should stick to the sides—be sure to coat all the sides and the bottom of the bowl with uncolored batter.

Working quickly, pour the pink/red batter into the center of the small metal mixing bowl, careful not to scrape the sides of the pan—some mixing bowls are smaller than others; try to only fill your bowl about two-thirds of the way. Any additional red batter can be made into cupcakes, and flat-iced with green frosting, streaked using the same method as the large cake (described below).

Bake for 45 minutes to 1 hour, checking often (the cake will take longer to cook because of its density). Completely cool the cake before decorating.

How to Decorate Wonderful Watermelon Cake

Sit your cooled cake upside down on a cake plate (the domed surface of the cake is now the top).

Tint your Basic Buttercream a pale yellowy-green using the green and yellow food coloring. Use it to flat-ice the cake—don't worry about getting the frosting too flat. Place one drop of green food coloring on your frosting spatula. Starting at the bottom of the cake, gently spread the food coloring up, careful not to mix the food coloring into the frosting.

Move over about an inch and repeat with a new drop of green food coloring. Continue repeating until the entire cake has a dark and light green mottled appearance.

Once your cake is striped green, refrigerate for about 10 minutes. Pull it out and smooth it using the parchment paper technique described in the Flat-Icing section of this book (page 17).

CUPCAKE-CAKEBALL COMBOS

What's better than a cupcake? Why, a cupcake with a cakeball on top, of course! Adding cakeballs to your cupcakes opens up a world of design possibilities and is perfect for those times when a single cupcake isn't enough.

Like the design, but want less cake? Simply remove about a teaspoon of batter from each cupcake before baking (approximately the amount needed for a cakeball) to get the look without as much cake—just remember to reduce your baking time accordingly: smaller cupcakes take less time to cook.

BABY TURTLES

These adorable little turtles on their sandy cupcake bases are almost too cute to eat.

You Will Need:

- 1 cake recipe, baked as 18 cupcakes + 18 cakeballs
- 1 recipe frosting of your choice
- yellow food coloring
- 1 cup white melting wafers
- 1 cup yellow melting wafers
- ½ teaspoon shortening
- double boiler or small microwavable bowl
- ½ teaspoon cocoa powder
- fork
- wax or parchment paper
- 1½ cups edible sand (page 38)
- spoon
- 54 green M&M's (plus some spares for mistakes)
- 9 green M&M's Minis
- sharp knife
- 1 tube black Decorator's Icing
- small round piping tip (#3) compatible with Decorator's Icing tube

How to Decorate Baby Turtle Cupcakes

Combine both colors of the melting wafers and the shortening in a small microwavable bowl or a double boiler and melt them until smooth.

Use a fork to dip the cakeballs in the melting wafer coating. Tap off any excess coating against the side of the bowl/pot, then sit the cakeballs on wax or parchment paper, and set them aside to harden.

Use cocoa powder and yellow food coloring to tint your frosting a light sandy yellow-brown. Flat-ice the cupcakes with it.

While the frosting is still wet, sprinkle the edible sand on top of the cupcakes with a spoon.

Use a sharp knife to cut 36 green M&M's and all the M&M's Minis in half.

Place a coated cakeball in the center of each cupcake. Gently nestle a full M&M into the "sand" on one side of the cakeball—this is your turtle's head. Place a half-M&M's Mini, cut-side down, at the opposite end of the cakeball—this is your turtle's tail.

Gently nestle two half-M&M's on their sides on each side of the turtle as his flippers. Press them into the sand to hide the cut edges. Do this for all 18 turtles.

Attach your small round compatible tip to your tube of black Decorator's Icing and pipe two small dots for eyes on each full M&M.

SPOOKY SPIDERS

These spooky treats are perfect for Halloween birthdays or any birthday kids who love creepy crawlies.

You Will Need:
- 1 cake recipe, baked as 18 cupcakes + 18 cakeballs
- 1 white frosting recipe
- 1 tube blue decorating gel
- blunt knife
- 2 cups purple melting wafers
- ¼ teaspoon shortening
- microwave-safe bowl or cup or a double boiler
- black licorice shoelace candy
- scissors
- 18 black gumdrops
- 36 small candy eyeballs
- 1 tube red Decorator's Icing
- small round tip (#3) compatible with Decorator's Icing tube

How to Decorate Spooky Spider Cupcakes
Flat-ice a cupcake with white frosting.

Using the decorating gel, pipe two circles on top of a cupcake, one inside the other.

Starting at the center of the cupcake, draw a knife across the cupcake to the outer edge.

Repeat this five more times, spaced around the cupcake.

Do this for all of the cupcakes.

Use scissors to cut your black licorice shoelace candy into 144 one-inch long pieces (8 pieces for each of the 18 cakeball spiders).

Place your melting wafers in the microwave or double boiler with the shortening and melt until smooth.

Dip one cakeball in the melted candy, and tap any excess off against the side of the bowl. Working quickly, sit the cakeball on top of the cupcake, at the back, and press four licorice pieces onto each side of the cakeball, letting their other ends touch the frosting.

If your coating hardens too fast, simply dip the ends of your licorice into your bowl/double boiler of coating, and attach them.

Dip the bottom of a gumdrop into the melted coating, and attach it to the front of the cakeball.

Dab a small amount of white frosting on the back of two candy eyeballs and attach them to the front of the gumdrop.

Attach your small round compatible tip to your tube of Decorator's Icing and pipe a smile under the eyes.

Repeat for the remaining cakeballs.

ICE CREAM SUNDAES

These ice cream sundaes are so realistic-looking, you'll want to serve them with spoons. Decorate them with plain melting wafers for a uniform white chocolate flavor, or use flavored melting wafers (and the extra flavoring listed in the recipe below) to make the sundaes actually taste like the ice cream flavors they're pretending to be.

You Will Need:

- 1 cake recipe, baked as 18 cupcakes + 18 cakeballs
- 1 recipe frosting of your choice
- 1 cup pink melting wafers (*optional:* strawberry melting wafers)
- 2 cups white melting wafers (*optional:* ¼ teaspoon vanilla + ¼ teaspoon peppermint extract)
- 1 teaspoon shortening

- double boiler or 4 small microwavable bowls
- fork
- blue and yellow liquid food coloring
- ¼ cup chocolate chips
- 18 red M&M's
- sprinkles
- spoons

How to Decorate Ice Cream Sundae Cupcakes

Flat-ice all of the cupcakes with your frosting. Don't worry about getting them too flat—you want them to look like ice cream.

Place pink (*optional:* strawberry) melting wafers and ¼ teaspoon shortening in a small microwavable bowl or double boiler and melt them until smooth. Use a fork to dip a cakeball and immediately place it on a cupcake—you want the coating to drip down a bit onto your cupcake. Do this for a total of 6 cupcakes.

Place 1 cup of white melting wafers, ¼ teaspoon shortening, and two drops of yellow food coloring in another small microwavable bowl or double boiler (if using the same double boiler, clean and dry it thoroughly before using it for the white wafers) and melt until smooth. (*Optional:* add ¼ teaspoon vanilla extract to the melting wafers.)

Use a fork to dip a cakeball in the yellowy-white coating and immediately place it on a cupcake—again, you want the coating to drip down onto the cupcake. Do this for a total of 6 cupcakes.

Place the remaining white melting wafers and ¼ teaspoon shortening into a small microwavable bowl or the double boiler and melt them until smooth. Add a few drops of blue and yellow food coloring to make a pale green color. (*Optional:* add ¼ teaspoon of peppermint extract.)

Use a fork to dip a cakeball and immediately place it on a cupcake, allowing the coating to drip down onto the cupcake. Do this for the remaining cakeballs and cupcakes.

Place your chocolate chips and the remaining shortening into a small microwavable bowl or double boiler and melt until smooth. Spoon about ½ teaspoon chocolate onto a cakeball, letting the chocolate drip about a quarter of the way down the sides of the cakeball.

While the chocolate is still wet, add 1 red M&M (writing side down) on the top of each cakeball, and use a spoon to add a few sprinkles to the chocolate. Repeat for the remaining cakeballs.

Optional: Serve in sundae bowls with spoons for a special treat.

BRILLIANT BEARS

These little bears are as sweet inside as they are out.

You Will Need:

- 1 cake recipe, baked as 22 cupcakes + 11 cakeballs
- 1 recipe Basic Buttercream (page 46) or Dreamy Cream Cheese Frosting (page 47)
- small bowl
- 3 tablespoons + ¼ teaspoon cocoa powder
- yellow food coloring
- ½ teaspoon water

- serrated knife
- 44 large candy eyeballs
- 44 milk chocolate melting wafers
- 22 large pink heart quins
- 1 tube black Decorator's Icing
- small round tip (#3) compatible with Decorator's Icing tube

How to Decorate Brilliant Bear Cupcakes

Scoop 1 cup frosting into a small bowl. Add ¼ teaspoon cocoa powder and a little bit of yellow food coloring to tint the frosting a light tan color.

Add 3 tablespoons cocoa and ½ teaspoon water to the remaining frosting. Use this chocolate frosting to flat-ice the cupcakes.

Slice each cakeball in half with your serrated knife.

Frost each half-cakeball with tan frosting. Place each half-cakeball cut-side down, on the top of each cupcake, below the center—this is your bear's snout.

Place 2 candy eyeballs on each cupcake, above the cakeball snout.

Press 2 chocolate melting wafers into each cupcake above the eyes—these are your bear's ears.

Place 1 large pink heart quin on the center of each cakeball snout.

Attach your small round compatible tip to the tube of black Decorator's Icing and pipe a "J" on the cakeball snout, starting at the heart nose, and coming down to the bottom of the cakeball. Pipe a small swooping line on the other side of the "J" to mirror it, and complete the bear's mouth.

MILLIONS OF MONSTERS

Perhaps the best thing about these mini monsters is the flexibility of design. You could make a dozen copies of the same monster or eighteen completely unique creations. Really, if you have enough candy (and patience) the options are limitless. Also, your cakeballs don't have to be perfect spheres—lumpy shapes help to give your monsters character.

You Will Need:
- 1 cake recipe, baked as 18 cupcakes + 18 cakeballs
- 1 recipe Basic Buttercream *(stiff consistency)* (page 46)
- Different-colored melting wafers or white chocolate (about ½ cup per 2–3 monsters) or a second recipe Basic Buttercream *(thin consistency)* (page 46)
- wax or parchment paper
- small, microwave-safe bowl or double boiler

Optional Ingredients:
- white melting wafers (eyes, teeth)
- M&M's Minis
- regular M&M's
- large candy eyeballs
- small candy eyeballs
- Good & Plenties (horns)
- jelly beans (horns)
- Starburst Minis, cut in half diagonally (spikes)
- colored coconut in the same colors as your melting wafers (see instructions on page 38)
- 1 tube of red or black Decorator's Icing (for mouths) + compatible small round tip

How to Decorate Millions of Monsters
If you are planning on making multiple colors of monsters, start with the lightest color first—that way you can mix darker colors into your leftover melted candy, cutting down on waste.

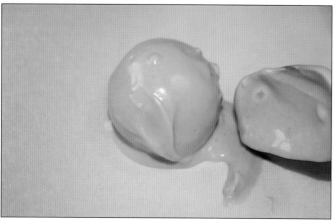

Melt ¾ cup of your lightest color melting wafers or white chocolate in either a microwave-safe bowl or a double boiler, and stir in ¼ teaspoon shortening. Using a spoon or fork, roll the cakeball in the melted coating. Tap your utensil against the side of the bowl to remove any excess coating. Place the cakeball on wax paper on a flat surface (cookie sheets work well) and decide which side is the best side. This will be your front/face. If you want, use the utensil to drag some of the pooling coating around from the back of the monster, making a tail.

Add spikes by dipping Starburst Mini halves into the melted coating.

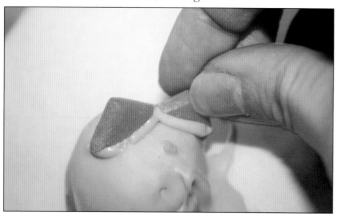

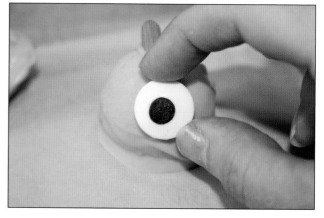

Apply the spikes to the monster in a stripe down its back. Hold each spike in place for 2–5 seconds until the coating hardens.

Spoon a little bit of wet coating onto a large candy eyeball and attach it to the front.

Hairy Monsters

Immediately after dipping a cakeball in the coating, roll it in the same color coconut.

While the coating is still soft, insert Good & Plenties down the monster's back as spikes.

Attach two jelly beans on the top of the cakeball, closest to the front. Dip the backs of two candy eyeballs in wet coating and attach them to the monster.

Cut a small triangle out of a white melting wafer and attach it under the eyes using wet coating. Using a tube of Decorator's Icing and your small round compatible tip, pipe a mouth on top of the tooth.

While you wait for your monsters to completely harden, frost your cupcakes. I recommend using tip #2D as it creates a flatter base for the monsters. If using one of the other tips, try to keep your icing flat rather than swirling up in the middle. Or skip the piping bag altogether and simply flat-ice your cupcakes.

Once the cupcakes are frosted, gently place one monster on top of each, pushing down slightly to anchor them.

Frosting-Only Monsters

Don't feel like dealing with candy wafers and/or coconut? Create hairy monsters with tip #233 (grass/hair tip). For frosting-only monsters, *start by frosting your cupcakes.*

Place one uncoated cakeball in the center of each frosted cupcake. Starting about ¼ inch above the bottom of the cakeball, pipe hair, pulling the piping bag down toward the cupcake. Release pressure on the bag and pull away as hair touches cupcake frosting.

Work your way around the cakeball. When you reach your starting point, move your piping tip up another ¼ inch and repeat step one, releasing pressure on the bag, and pulling away when your tip hits the first line of frosted hair.

Continue until your whole monster is covered in hair. Add candy horns, spikes, eyes, and/or mouths as per the instructions for the candy-coated monsters.

3-D DAZZLERS

These fabulous cakes stand on their own and are sure to put a smile on any birthday kid's face.

Using simple stacking and rearranging techniques and the magic of frosting, regular square, Bundt, loaf, and mixing bowl cakes are transformed into easy-to-assemble 3-D masterpieces that will leave your guests wondering if you used a specialty pan.

From gifts to baskets, critters to castles, there's sure to be a 3-D design to please any birthday kid or kid at heart.

PRETTY PRESENT

What's a birthday party without presents? With this gorgeous gift as your cake, you'll be able to have your present and eat it, too.

You Will Need:

- 1 cake recipe, baked in two 8-inch square pans
- 1 recipe filling (or use some of your yellow frosting)
- 1 recipe Basic Buttercream (page 46)
- 3 red Fruit by the Foot
- piping bag or large plastic bag + large round tip (#12)
- yellow food coloring
- 1 tube red Decorator's Icing
- large round tip (#12) compatible with Decorator's Icing
- 10–20 red, blue, and green jumbo star quins

How to Decorate Pretty Present Cake

Cut twelve to fifteen 3-inch strips of Fruit by the Foot.

Peel off the backing and roll it into a tube.

Fold the Fruit by the Foot over the tube of backing, and stick it shut on itself, forming a loop. (If the candy isn't sticky enough, you can use a dot of red Decorator's Icing, or wet with a single drop of water—just be careful not to get it too wet or the candy will melt.)

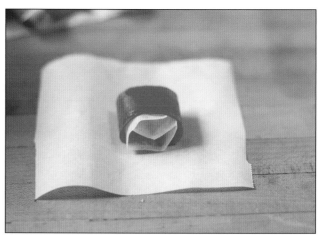

Sit the loop on a piece of wax or parchment paper to dry out. Repeat with all but one of your 3-inch strips of Fruit by the Foot. Set them aside to dry out.

For the last piece of Fruit by the Foot, peel off the backing and roll it into a tube. Roll the Fruit by the Foot into a circle around the backing tube, and stick it shut to itself. *This will be your center loop*. Sit it to dry with the others.

Tint your Basic Buttercream bright yellow. Scoop 1 cup of yellow frosting into a piping bag or plastic bag along with your large round tip (#12).

Level the cake and use the yellow frosting to pipe a dam. Fill with your desired filling, and assemble the cake.

Clean and dry your large round tip.

Use the yellow frosting to crumb-coat and flat-ice the cake.

Starting at the bottom center of one side of the cake, run the Fruit by the Foot up the side of the cake, across the top, and down the other side. Cut off any excess Fruit by the Foot.

Starting at the bottom center of one of the empty sides, run the Fruit by the Foot up the side, across the top (you will cross the other Fruit by the Foot) and down the opposite side to the bottom. Cut off any excess Fruit by the Foot.

Place red, green, and blue jumbo stars around the present, leaving space around where the ribbons cross. Press them gently in, until they are flush with the frosting.

How to Make the Bow

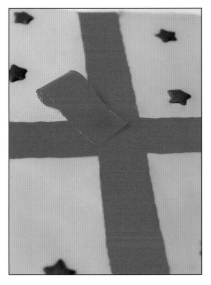

Using a small dot of red decorator's frosting, attach a loop on top of the cake beside where the two Fruit by the Foot ribbons cross.

Continue adding loops until you have a circle of them (6–7 loops).

Add a blob of Decorator's Icing to the center of the circle.

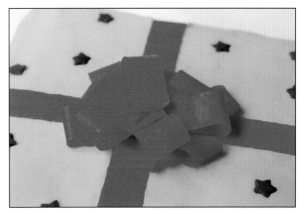

Attach a second layer of loops, placing each new loop between two of the first layer's loops.

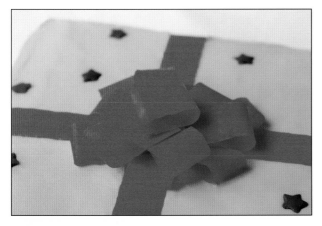

Add another dot of Decorator's Icing to the center and attach your final circle loop in the center of the bow.

UNBELIEVABLE UFO

Your guests will be over the moon for this space-age cake. For an extra-terrestrial treat, serve on a pedestal plate with glow sticks or LEDs taped underneath.

You Will Need:

- 1 cake recipe, baked in one 9-inch pie plate + 1 small metal mixing bowl
- 1 recipe Basic Buttercream (page 46)
- black, green, and red food coloring
- 9 orange Life Savers candies
- 9 blue M&M's
- 20 silver dragées
- 6 yellow Mike & Ike candies
- 1 green shoelace candy
- 1 old-fashioned hard candy stick (or substitute your candle for the UFO's antenna)
- sharp knife
- cutting board
- tweezers

How to Decorate Unbelievable UFO Cake

Use black, green, and red food coloring to tint the frosting gray.

Level both cakes. Place the pie plate cake upside down on the serving plate (the part that baked in the pan should be facing up).

Crumb-coat and flat-ice this base cake with gray frosting.

Place the mixing bowl cake upside down in the center of the pie plate cake. Crumb-coat and flat-ice the mixing bowl cake.

Place the orange Life Savers on the sides of the pie plate cake, spaced about 2 inches apart.

Center a blue M&M between each of the Life Savers.

Use tweezers to carefully place silver dragées on top of the pie plate cake, halfway between the edge of the cake and the mixing bowl cake.

Use your sharp knife to slice the Mike & Ike candies in half lengthwise—be very careful; the candies tend to roll. *(Younger bakers should get help from an adult.)*

Place the half-candies in pairs on the side of the mixing bowl cake, spaced about ¼-inch from each other and 1½ inches from the next pair.

Measure a piece of green shoelace candy around the widest part of the mixing bowl you baked your cake in. Cut it to this length. Starting at the back of the cake (so the seam is hidden) carefully place the shoelace candy around the base of the mixing bowl cake.

Place your old-fashioned hard candy (or candle) in the center of the top of the mixing bowl cake.

BASKET OF BERRIES

Made with a chocolate basketweave pattern and fresh berries, this clever cake tastes even better than it looks.

You Will Need:

- 1 recipe Pound Cake (page 41) or Cake Mix Fix (page 43), baked as one 8-inch round + 1 medium (8-inch diameter) metal mixing bowl
- 1 recipe Basic Buttercream, chocolate variation (page 46)
- piping bag
- 1 coupler and ring
- basketweave tip (#47)
- wax or parchment paper
- cookie sheet or extra plate (minimum 8-inch diameter)
- serving plate
- large star tip (#21)
- 2 cups fresh berries, hulled, pitted, and/or de-stemmed

How to Assemble and Decorate Basket of Berries Cake

Note: This cake is assembled and frosted upside down, then flipped before adding the berries.

Scoop 1 cup chocolate buttercream into a piping bag with the coupler and basketweave tip (#47).

Place a sheet of wax or parchment paper on your cookie sheet or large plate.

Level cakes so they are flat. **Note:** For the mixing bowl cake you are trimming off the excess that puffed up on the open side of the cake—the bottom of the cake should remain domed (i.e., shaped like the bowl it was baked in).

Place the 8-inch round cake on wax/parchment paper with the cut (leveled) side facing up. Pipe a dam and fill the cake (I suggest using your chocolate buttercream).

Carefully place the mixing bowl cake cut-side down (domed side up) onto the filling.

Use your piping bag to pipe a basketweave pattern on the cake (instructions on page 28).

Once your basketweave pattern is complete, daub or squeeze some frosting on the top of the cake. Center the plate you will be serving your cake on over the top of the cake and place it upside down onto the cake.

Note: Younger bakers, or those with smaller hands, may need help with the following step.

Very carefully, grasp the sides of the two plates (or plate and cookie sheet) with both hands—as if you were picking up an extra-large sandwich.

Turn your hands away from you, flipping the cake, so the serving plate is now on the bottom. Gently sit it down.

Remove the cookie sheet/top plate and wax/parchment paper.

Flat-ice the top of the cake with chocolate buttercream.

Remove your basketweave tip from the piping bag and replace it with your large star tip (#21). Pipe a line around the top edge of the cake.

Cover the top of the cake with fresh berries.

Note: Because of the berries, the cake and any leftovers should be stored in the refrigerator.

PICNIC BASKET

This stunning basketweave cake is the perfect dessert for a summer picnic party—just don't forget to pack the forks. **Note:** These cakes are assembled right-side up (they will sit on the serving plate the same way they sat in the pan to bake).

You Will Need:

- 1 cake recipe, baked in two loaf pans
- 1 recipe Basic Buttercream (page 46)
- 2 piping bags
- petal tip (#103)
- 1 tablespoon cocoa powder
- yellow food coloring
- large star tip (#21)
- 1 coupler and ring
- large serrated knife
- cutting board
- 3 double-wide graham crackers
- basketweave tip (#47)
- 1 tube red Decorator's Icing
- petal tip (#103) compatible with Decorator's Icing tube
- strawberries and grapes (or your choice of small fruit)

How to Assemble and Decorate Perfect Picnic Basket Cake

Scoop 1 cup Basic Buttercream into a piping bag with your petal tip. Set it aside.

Stir 1 tablespoon cocoa powder and yellow food coloring into the remaining Basic Buttercream, until the frosting reaches the color of a graham cracker. Place 1 cup of this frosting into a piping bag with a coupler and the large star tip (#21).

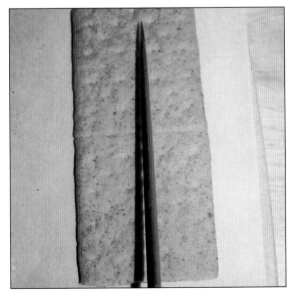

Cut one of your graham crackers in half lengthwise (along the seam, if there is one).

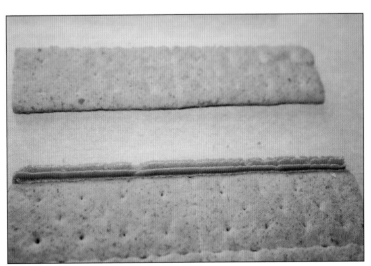

Use your piping bag with the star tip to pipe a line of frosting onto the edge of a full graham cracker.

Press one of the graham cracker halves into the frosting. Repeat with other graham crackers and set both aside to harden.

To assemble this cake, sit one loaf cake right-side up on a cutting board and use your large serrated knife to cut about a ½ inch off the long side of the cake, removing the beveled edge (loaf pans are smaller at the bottom than the top). Do the same to the other loaf cake.

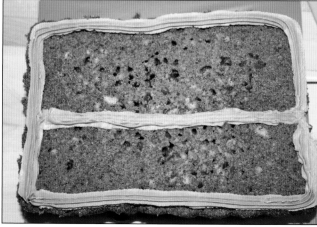

Spread a small amount of graham cracker-colored frosting on the cut edge of one of the cakes.

Sit the two cakes on a serving plate, cut edges together, and press them gently together with your hands.

If you want to fill your cake, use your serrated knife to torte the cake (see instructions on torting on page 8) and pipe your dam so it fills the crack between the two cakes, as well as around the outside edge.

Once your cake has been filled and reassembled, you are ready to start your basketweave. Remove the large star tip from the piping bag and replace it with the basketweave tip. Cover all four sides of the cake with a basketweave pattern (see instructions on page 28).

Once all four sides are covered in basketweave, flat-ice two-thirds of the top of the cake with graham cracker-colored frosting, leaving one-third of the cake near one of the ends bare. Don't worry about getting it perfect; this frosting will be covered.

Remove the basketweave tip from the piping bag and replace it with the large star tip (#21). Pipe a line around the top edge of the basketweave pattern.

Carefully place one of your extra-wide graham crackers on top of the cake, flush to the edge of the fully-frosted end.

If any of the flat-iced area is exposed around the edges, use your star tip to fill it in.

Take your piping bag of white frosting and pipe a large "V" from the bare side of the cake, over the edge, making sure to anchor it to the basketweave frosting. Do the same for both sides of the cake, making the top of the "V" as wide as the unfrosted area.

Once the entire area has been filled in with white frosting, attach your compatible petal tip to your tube of red Decorator's Icing (if reusing the same tip, make sure to clean and dry it thoroughly before attaching).

Starting at the tip of one of the triangles, pipe a red square on top of the frosting.

Continue piping red squares in a checkerboard pattern—starting each red square at the corner of the one before it. Repeat until the entire white area is covered in checkerboard.

Place fruit on top of checkerboard area. Place the remaining extra-wide graham cracker on top of the fruit, so one edge touches the middle of the picnic basket.

Remove the star tip from your piping bag and replace it with the basketweave tip. Holding the bag so the flat side of the tip is up (serrated side is down) pipe lines over the gap between the two graham crackers.

COLORFUL CATERPILLAR

This adorable creepy-crawly cake will have kids lining up to take a bite.

You Will Need:

- 1 recipe Pound Cake (page 41) or Cake Mix Fix (page 43), baked in a Bundt pan
- large serrated knife
- 12 x 15-inch cake plate (or cookie sheet)
- 1 recipe Basic Buttercream (page 46)
- red, blue, and yellow food coloring

- 6 medium bowls
- 26 black jelly beans
- 1 black licorice shoelace candy
- 2 large candy eyeballs
- 1 piping bag and small round tip (#3) or small plastic bag with the corner cut off

How to Decorate Colorful Caterpillar Cake

De-pan your cake. For this design, the bottom of the cake (the part that was baked in the pan) will be the top of the finished cake.

Using a large serrated knife, cut the Bundt cake exactly in half. Position the two halves on your cake platter or cookie sheet so they form a backward "S" shape.

Trim a little off one end of the cake to round out the edges. This will be your head.

Separate your frosting into the six bowls, and tint one each of the following colors: green, blue, purple, red, orange, and yellow.

Flat-ice the head with green frosting. (My Bundt pan has alternating large and small bumps, so I frosted a large and a small bump together as a single color—if your pan only has one size bumps, frost each bump a different color.) You may need to use a piping bag (or a bag with the corner cut off) to help frost the cut edges of the cake.

Flat-ice the next section of your caterpillar blue.

Continue flat-icing sections of the caterpillar following the color spectrum (after blue is purple, then red, orange, yellow, and back to green) until the entire cake is flat-iced.

Place thirteen black jelly beans sticking out from under the edge of each side of the cake, as feet.

Cut two 3-inch strips of black licorice shoelace, and poke each into the top of the head to form antennae.

Using a bit of green frosting, attach the two candy eyeballs to the front of the head.

Place a small amount of red frosting into a piping bag with a small round tip (#3) or into a small plastic bag with the corner cut off, and pipe a smile below the caterpillar's eyes.

SLITHERING SNAKE

Completely covered in crunchy M&M's "scales," this yummy cake gives a whole new meaning to the word *snakebite*.

You Will Need:

- 1 cake recipe, baked in a Bundt pan
- 12 x 15-inch cake plate (or cookie sheet)
- 1 recipe Basic Buttercream (page 46)
- green food coloring
- 4 cups green M&M's

- ½ cup green M&M's Minis
- ½ cup orange M&M's
- 2 large candy eyeballs
- 1 strawberry Fruit by the Foot

How to Decorate Slithering Snake Cake

Cut, position, and trim your cake according to the instructions in Caterpillar Cake (page 153).

Trim off some of the tail end of your cake, to form a point. Tint your basic buttercream green.

Beginning at the tail, flat-ice a portion of the cake—if the frosting isn't sticking well to the cut edges, use a piping bag and the large petal tip (#103) to help cover the cut edges. Only flat-ice a small section of the cake at a time, so the frosting will stay wet enough to hold the M&M's in place.

While the frosting is still wet, place green M&M's on it in a bricklay pattern, starting at the tip of the tail. Use M&M's Minis to fill in any gaps between the larger M&M's.

After approximately four rows of green M&M's, place a diamond of orange M&M's (one M&M, followed by two, followed by three, then two, then one) on the back of the snake.

Fill in around it with green M&M's.

Place another four complete rows of green M&M's. Repeat the orange diamond and continue repeating them after every four complete rows of green M&M's until the cake is completely covered.

Once the entire snake is covered in M&M's, use a small dot of frosting to attach the candy eyeballs to the front of the head.

Cut a 3-inch long Y-shape out of strawberry Fruit by the Foot, and place it at the front of the snake as its tongue.

WHITE CHOCOLATE CASTLE

I'm not a big fan of ice cream cones (at least, not when there's no ice cream inside them), so I wanted to create a castle design that didn't call for them. This medieval-inspired castle uses white chocolate for its crenellations and chocolate bars and chocolate cookies for its details.

You Will Need:

- 1 cake recipe, baked as two 8-inch square pans, + 4 cupcakes (baked without liners)
- 1 frosting recipe*
- 1 recipe filling of your choice (or use some of your frosting)

- 2 large white chocolate bars
- 1 Kit Kat bar
- 6 chocolate-covered finger cookies
- ⅔ cup candy-covered chocolate rocks or pebbles

*I recommend using ½ butter or margarine, and regular—not clear—vanilla extract to try to match the color of your white chocolate—if necessary you can also add a drop or two or yellow food coloring to help match the color.

How to Decorate White Chocolate Castle

Level, fill, assemble, crumb-coat, and flat-ice your two 8-inch square layers.

Place your four cupcakes upside down on top of the cake, one in each corner, slightly away from the sides of the cake—if your cupcakes require a crumb coat, I suggest you do this before placing them on the cake.

Flat-ice the cupcakes.

Cut your white chocolate bar along the lines, into squares or rectangles.

Place the white chocolate rectangles on their side, on top of the outside edge of the cake, printed side facing in, to form castle crenellations.

Cut five white chocolate rectangles in half.

Place the half-size chocolate rectangles on top of the cupcakes, along their outside edges.

Break off two fingers of Kit Kat bar. Slice them in half.

Gently press the two halves on the front side of the cake, writing side out, immediately next to each other, to form a door.

Cut about a ½ inch off the rounded ends of the chocolate covered finger cookies. Gently press one, flat-side out, on each side of the door.

Press two on each side of the castle, and one each onto the cupcake turrets on top of the cake. Place the candy-coated chocolate pebbles or rocks around the bottom edge of the cake to hide the messy edge where it meets the serving plate.

TASTY TREASURE CHEST

This chocolate-covered treat is perfect for pirate parties. If the number of chocolate bars scares you off, consider making just one half of the chest and baking the rest of the batter in a pie plate—simply frost the pie plate cake and cover it with edible sand to use it as the base for your tasty treasure chest.

You Will Need:

- 1 cake recipe, baked in 2 loaf pans
- 1 frosting recipe
- yellow and red food coloring
- small bowl
- ½ cup yellow sugar
- 16 Kit Kat bars
- 10 Fruit Gushers gems
- 2 tablespoons cocoa powder
- 1 roll Color by the Foot Fruit by the Foot candy
- 2 tablespoons white pearl sprinkles
- tweezers

How to Decorate Tasty Treasure Chest

Place one cake right-side up (the way it baked in the pan) at the front of your serving plate.

Scoop 1 cup frosting into a small bowl and stir yellow and one drop of red food coloring into frosting until it reaches a deep gold color. Flat-ice the top of the cake—don't worry about getting it too perfect, as it will be covered. Sprinkle a thick layer of yellow sugar on top of the frosting.

Measure one of your Kit Kat bars, standing on its end, against the side of the cake. If your cake is shorter than the bar, trim the bar so it is about ¼ inch taller than the cake. Use this bar as a guide to cut 8 bars to the proper length.

Stir 2 tablespoons cocoa powder into the remaining uncolored frosting. Use this to flat-ice one side of the cake—again, don't worry about perfection, this will also be covered. While the frosting is still wet, stand the Kit Kats up against the side of the cake (cut-side down, writing-side out) and gently press them into the frosting.

Flat-ice the other sides of the cake and attach the Kit Kats to those sides as well.

Before placing the second cake on the serving plate, flat-ice one long side of the cake with chocolate frosting. While the frosting is still wet, sit two Kit Kats (on their sides this time) against the side of the cake and gently press them into the frosting.

Carefully move the second cake onto the serving plate so the Kit Kat–covered side is up against the back of the first cake.

Flat-ice the top of the second cake with chocolate frosting, but otherwise leave it plain.

Flat-ice the remaining sides with chocolate frosting and cover them with KitKats sitting sideways.

Scatter Fruit Gusher gems on top of the yellow sugar on the first cake.

Using tweezers, carefully place white pearl sprinkles in round lines, forming bracelets.

Cut a 1-inch piece of yellow Fruit by the Foot. Carefully cut a keyhole shape out of the center of the candy. Daub a small amount of gold frosting on the back of the Fruit by the Foot and gently press it onto the center of the front of the treasure chest.

MARVELOUS MONSTER

With his spiky fur and colorful toenails, this adorable monster is as cute as he is tasty.

You Will Need:

- 1 pound cake recipe (or Cake Mix Fix, page 43) baked in a small metal mixing bowl + one 6-inch round cake + 9 cakeballs
- 1 recipe Basic Buttercream (page 46)
- 1 recipe filling of choice (or use orange or green frosting)
- ⅓ cup white chocolate melting wafers
- ½ teaspoon shortening
- double boiler or 2 small microwavable bowl
- medium-size bowl
- green, yellow, and red food coloring
- 2 piping bags
- 2 couplers and rings
- fork or skewer
- 3 yellow M&M's (+ extras to cover breakage)
- 1 cup orange melting wafers
- wax or parchment paper
- grass/hair piping tip (#233)
- large round tip (#12)
- 3 brown M&M's
- 1 tube red Decorator's Icing
- small round tip (#3) compatible with Decorator's Icing tube

How to Decorate Marvelous Monster Cake

Melt the white chocolate melting wafers and ¼ teaspoon shortening together with a double boiler or using a small microwavable bowl and microwave.

Stick a fork or skewer into a cakeball and dip the top (the most rounded part) into the white chocolate melting wafers. Tap the fork on the outside of the bowl to remove the excess, then sit the cakeball on wax or parchment paper to harden. Repeat with two more cakeballs.

Slice the yellow M&M's in half.

Melt the orange wafers in another small microwavable bowl or double boiler. (If using the double boiler, be certain to thoroughly clean and dry it before use.)

Stick a fork into a fresh cakeball and coat it entirely in orange candy. Tap off any excess against the side of the bowl. While the coating is still wet, gently press the point of half a yellow M&M into the side of the cakeball, cut-side facing down. Repeat this for the remaining five plain cakeballs. Leave on wax/parchment paper to harden.

Stick a fork, skewer, or toothpick into the exposed side of one of the white-coated cakeballs. Dip the cakeball's bottom (the part that touches the table when sitting flat), the sides, and just a bit of the top into the orange melts. Repeat for two remaining white cakeballs.

Scoop half of the Basic Buttercream frosting into a medium-size bowl and tint it green. Place it in a piping bag with a coupler and the large round tip (#12). Squeeze a large dot into the center of the white area of one of the white and orange cakeballs.

Place a brown M&M in the middle of the green dot. Repeat with the two remaining white and orange cakeballs. Leave them on the wax/parchment paper to set. Tint the other half of the Basic Buttercream orange with your yellow and red food coloring.

Level the two cakes. Place the 6-inch round cake on a serving plate, cut-side down. Using your green frosting, pipe a dam, and fill it with your desired filling.

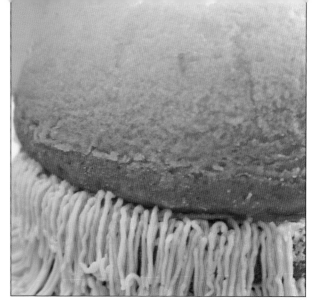

Remove the large round tip from the green frosting bag and replace it with the grass/hair tip (#233). Starting half an inch above the bottom of the cake, hold your piping bag at a 90° angle, and pipe hair down toward the cake plate, releasing when you touch the plate.

Place orange frosting in a piping bag with a coupler and the grass/hair tip. Starting half an inch above the green hair frosting, pipe orange hair down, releasing when you reach the green frosting hair. Continue piping orange hair around the body of the monster until you reach your starting point.

Nestle three orange cakeballs into the hair on either side of the front of the cake.

Remove the grass/hair tip, wash and thoroughly dry it. Re-couple the tip on the piping bag of green frosting. Starting half an inch above the orange frosting hair, pipe green frosting down, releasing when you reach the orange frosting hair. Continue piping green hair around until you reach your starting.

Continue alternating layers of orange and green hair, thoroughly rinsing and drying piping tip in between layers, until the entire cake is covered in frosting hair.

Stick a toothpick into base of each eye cakeball and use them to anchor the eyes on the top of the cake. **Note:** Be sure to remove toothpicks when serving the cake.

Attach the small round compatible tip to the tube of red Decorator's Icing and pipe a wavy smile across the cake between the eyes and the toes.

CREATIVE CUTOUTS

With a few simple cuts, these cakes transform from regular round and rectangular shapes into fun and creative creations. A stable cake is a must for these designs, so be sure to use a pound cake variation (without pieces of fruit) (page 42) or the Cake Mix Fix recipe (page 43).

These cakes also end up larger than your average cake once assembled. Most cake decorating stores sell cake boards in extra-large sizes. If you don't want to go to the expense, feel free to use a cookie sheet or platter. For a more festive look, consider covering your cookie sheet with a plastic tablecloth before assembling the cake on it.

RADICAL ROBOT

This mechanical cake is so cute, you almost won't want to eat him.

You Will Need:

- 1 recipe Pound Cake (page 41) or Cake Mix Fix (page 43), baked as one 9 x 13-inch rectangular pan, + 5 mini cupcakes (baked without wrappers)
- large cutting board
- serrated knife
- extra-large cake board or serving tray (assembled robot measures 22 inches long, 10 inches wide)
- 1 recipe Basic Buttercream (page 46)
- yellow, red, and blue food coloring
- 1 small bowl
- 2 piping bags
- 2 couplers and rings
- large petal tip (#103)

- 4 orange Starburst Minis
- 4 red Starburst Minis
- 2 yellow Starburst Minis
- 4 orange M&M's
- 2 large candy eyeballs
- 1 red Life Saver
- 1 yellow juicy gel candy
- 1 orange or blue old-fashioned hard candy stick
- 2 tablespoons silver dragées
- tweezers
- 1 tube black Decorator's Icing
- 1 small round tip (#3) compatible with Decorator's Icing tube

How to Decorate Radical Robot Cake

Use your serrated knife to cut the 9 x 13-inch cake according to the diagram. Template and diagrams can be found at the back of this book.

Sit the head piece on your cake board/serving tray, leaving three inches between the top of the head and the edge of the tray.

Scoop 1½ cups Basic Buttercream into a small bowl and use the yellow and red food coloring to tint it orange. Scoop about half of it into a piping bag with a coupler. Set it aside.

Tint the remaining uncolored Basic Buttercream blue. Scoop 1 cup into a piping bag with a coupler and the large petal tip. Pipe lines of frosting onto the cut edges of the head piece.

Use your spatula to smooth the frosting when finished. Flat-ice the rest of the head blue.

Remove the petal tip and clean and dry it thoroughly.

Place the neck pieces at the bottom of the head.

Attach the petal tip to the bag of orange frosting and pipe lines onto the neck. Use your spatula to smooth the frosting when done.

Remove, clean, and dry the petal tip and replace it on the bag of blue frosting. Before moving the robot's body into place, pipe lines of blue frosting across the top edge of the cake, and smooth it with a spatula.

Place the robot's body under its neck. Pipe frosting onto the cut edges, and smooth them with a spatula. Flat-ice the remaining body areas.

Place the legs on the cake board, at the bottom of the body.

Remove, clean, and dry the petal tip, and replace it on the bag of orange frosting. Pipe orange frosting onto the cut edges of the legs only—leave the feet bare—and smooth it with a spatula. Flat-ice the remaining areas of the legs only.

Cut one-third off of one side of three mini cupcakes. Place one cupcake upside-down on the top side of the robot's head, cut-side down on the plate. Place another, also cut-side down, at each of the robot's shoulders.

Cut small triangles out of two mini cupcakes, as shown. Place one mini cupcake at the end of each arm.

Carefully, pipe orange frosting onto the three mini cupcakes, and smooth with a spatula.

Remove, clean, and dry the petal tip, and replace it on the bag of blue frosting. Pipe blue frosting onto the cut edges of the feet. Flat-ice the remaining feet areas.

Place one robot arm under each of the mini cupcake-shoulders, and pipe blue frosting onto the cut edges. Smooth over with a spatula. Flat-ice the remaining arm areas.

Remove, clean, and dry the petal tip and replace it on the bag of orange frosting. Pipe orange frosting onto the mini cupcakes, and smooth it over with a spatula.

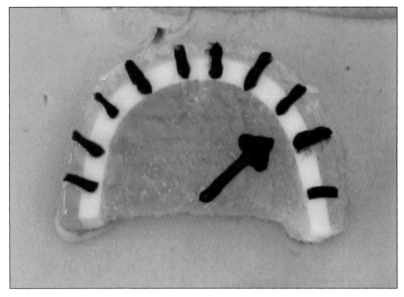

Pipe a large orange rectangle on the robot's body, about half an inch from the edges of his body. Inside the rectangle, about ¼ inch above the bottom line, place four Starburst Minis, alternating yellow and orange. Place the four M&M's in two columns, about ¼ inch above the two right-hand Starburst Minis. Center the red Life Saver to the left of the M&M's. Center the yellow juicy gel candy above the M&M's and Life Saver.

Place the compatible small round tip onto the tube of black Decorator's Icing, and pipe small lines around the outside edge of the juicy gel candy. Pipe a small arrow going from the bottom center of the candy, pointing toward one of the lines.

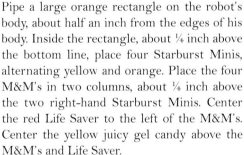

Place the two candy eyeballs on the robot's face. Place the four red mini Starburst candies in a line below them.

Cut the remaining two orange mini Starburst into three pieces each, and place them on the robot's feet as shoelaces.

Cut the old-fashioned hard candy in half, and push it into the mini cupcake on top of the robot's head.

Using tweezers, place a line of silver dragées, about ¼ inch apart, along orange rectangle, at the top and bottom of each leg, and on each shoulder. Place one dragée at the bottom of each arm (just above hand).

FESTIVE FLAMINGO

I designed this cake for a friend's daughter who made the rather specific request of a flamingo holding balloons. He turned out so cute, I couldn't resist including him here.

You Will Need:

- 1 recipe Pound Cake (page 41) or Cake Mix Fix (page 43) (baking directions can be found below)
- 9 x 13-inch rectangular pan + 8-inch round pan
- 5–6 cakeballs
- serrated knife
- parchment paper
- pen or marker
- scissors
- 1 recipe Basic Buttercream (page 46)
- blue, red, and yellow food coloring
- 2 piping bags
- 2 couplers and rings

- grass and hair tip (#233)
- small petal tip (#101)
- large round tip (#12)
- small star tip (#16)
- 2 small bowls
- ½ teaspoon cocoa powder
- red, blue, orange, and green melting wafers (about ¼ cup of each color) or 1 cup of white chocolate, divided + liquid food coloring
- 1 teaspoon shortening
- 4 small microwave-safe bowls or double boiler
- 1 brown M&M's Mini
- black licorice shoelace candy

How to Bake Festive Flamingo Cake

Preheat oven to 350°F. Spread about 1 cup of cake batter into 8-inch round pan (you want the batter to just cover the bottom of the pan). Bake for 8–10 minutes.

Note: There should be enough cake scraps after cutting to make the cakeballs using the frosting-and-crumbled-cake method; however, if you'd rather bake cakeballs, scoop out enough batter for 5–6 cakeballs before filling the 9 x 13-inch pan.

Pour the remaining batter into a 9 x 13-inch pan and bake at 350°F for 25–30 minutes.

Cool cakes completely before cutting.

How to Decorate Festive Flamingo Cake

Scoop 1½ cups of Basic Buttercream into a small bowl and tint it sky blue.

Place your 9 x 13-inch cake on a large serving plate. If you wish to torte and fill it, use some of your blue frosting in a piping bag, with the large round (#12) tip to pipe your dam. Clean and dry the bag and tip after use. If you want to use frosting as your filling, tint an extra 1½ cups frosting blue to fill; otherwise spread the filling of your choice inside the dam, and reassemble the cake.

Use the remaining blue frosting to flat-ice three-quarters of the cake, leaving the bottom quarter unfrosted.

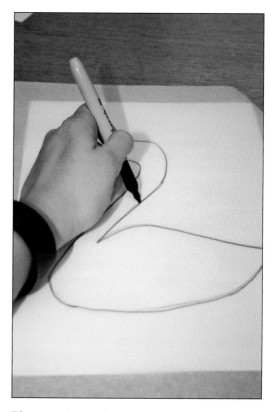

Place a piece of parchment paper over the flamingo and hat outlines in the back of this book and trace over them with a marker or pen. Cut out the flamingo and hat outlines from the wax/parchment paper.

Scoop ¾ cup frosting into a small bowl and use blue and yellow food coloring to tint it green. Place the green frosting into a piping bag with a coupler and the grass and hair tip (#233). Pipe grass across the unfrosted quarter of the cake.

Set the cake aside.

Place the wax/parchment paper flamingo and hat onto your 8-inch round cake and cut around them with a serrated knife.

Carefully sit the flamingo and hat onto the blue area of cake, leaving room for his legs at the bottom—it's okay if the flamingo's tail hangs over the base cake a little, just be careful when frosting it not to push too hard and break it off.

Scoop 1 cup frosting into a bowl and tint it pink with red food coloring (for a more authentic flamingo color, try adding 1–2 drops of yellow). Place ½ cup pink frosting into a piping bag with a coupler and the small petal tip (#101). Pipe along the cut edges of the flamingo, leaving his beak area unfrosted. Flat-ice the remaining flamingo body and neck pink—still leaving his beak unfrosted.

Remove the petal tip and replace it with the large round tip. Pipe a straight line from the flamingo's body down to the grass. Pipe a triangle at the end—you can smooth it with a finger after about 5–10 minutes once a crust forms.

Pipe a second leg starting beside the first, but going out at a 45° angle toward the flamingo's rear end, about 1 inch long. Change direction and continue piping the leg parallel to the grass, until you reach the first leg. Resume piping on the other side of the first leg, piping about ½ inch, before forming another triangle foot (again, wait 5–10 minutes, then smooth it over with a finger).

Carefully frost the upper half of the flamingo's beak white with uncolored frosting. Bring a small circle of white frosting up onto the pink area.

Place the brown M&M's Mini on the white circle.

Mix ½ teaspoon cocoa powder into 1 tablespoon of the remaining frosting, turning it dark brown. Frost the tip of the flamingo's beak with it.

Mix together 1 teaspoon blue frosting and 1 teaspoon pink frosting to form purple (if the color isn't dark enough, add a bit more food coloring to the mix). Flat-ice the hat purple.

Remove the grass and hair tip from the bag of green frosting and replace it with the small star tip (#16). Pipe a row of green stars across the bottom of the hat. Pipe a few scattered stars on the hat. Pipe one larger star on the tip of the hat.

Use the microwave or a double boiler to melt one color of melting wafers at a time. Stir ¼ teaspoon of shortening into the melted coating, and dip one or two cakeballs in each color. Sit them on parchment paper to harden.

Once hardened, sit the cakeballs on the cake up by the flamingo's head.

Cut the black licorice shoelaces into 6-inch strips. Carefully place the licorice strings under the edges of the cakeballs, running down to the flamingo's extended foot.

Cut a 1-inch piece of black licorice shoelace and tie it in a loose knot. Sit it on the flamingo's foot—if it won't stay, use a dot of brown frosting to hold it in place.

FANTASTIC FISH

This gorgeous fishy cake will swim its way into your heart—and your belly.

You Will Need:
- 1 recipe Pound Cake (page 41) or Cake Mix Fix (page 43), baked in a 9 x 13-inch rectangular pan
- large serrated knife
- large cutting board
- 12 x 15-inch cake board or covered cookie sheet
- 1 recipe Basic Buttercream (page 46)
- yellow and red food coloring
- 1 piping bag
- large petal tip (#103)
- 1 cup orange melting wafers
- 1 cup purple melting wafers
- 1 cup light blue melting wafers
- 1 cup dark blue melting wafers
- 1 white chocolate melting wafer
- 1 brown M&M's Mini
- 1 red Hot Lips candy
- 1 sugared orange slice candy

How to Decorate Fantastic Fish Cake
Note: If you want to torte and fill this cake, do so after cutting, to prevent leakage.

Place the de-panned cake right-side up on a large cutting board. Use your serrated knife to cut cake according to the diagram at the back of this book.

Arrange the cake on your serving tray as pictured in the photo. Note that the upper piece of the tail needs to be flipped upside down to fit properly. Trim a bit off the tail so it forms a curved edge.

Using your yellow and red food coloring, tint the frosting a similar shade of orange as your orange melting wafers.

Put your small petal tip (#103) into a piping bag and fill it with frosting. Use this to pipe frosting onto the cut edges of the cake. Use a spatula to smooth over the frosting on the cut edges of the tail, but don't worry about smoothing over the body, since it will be covered in scales.

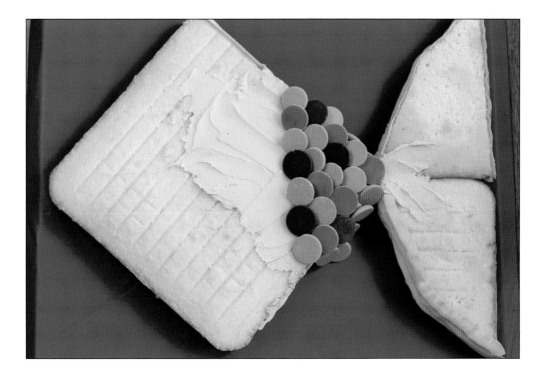

Starting where the tail attaches, flat-ice a small portion of the diamond-shaped cake. Place orange, purple, light blue, and dark blue melting wafers on the frosted area of the cake in a bricklay pattern, alternating the colors randomly. You want to make sure to only frost a small patch at a time, so the frosting stays wet enough for the candy wafers to stick to it.

Continue frosting and placing melting wafers, until the entire diamond-shaped cake, *except the front tip*, is covered with candy wafers.

Attach your red Hot Lips candy to the front tip of the cake.

Using a small amount of your orange frosting as glue, attach your white melting wafer, above and to the right of the lips. Use a dot of frosting to attach the brown M&M's Mini to the center of the white melting wafer.

Use a rolling pin to flatten the orange slice candy—if you don't have a rolling pin, simply place a piece of wax or parchment paper on top of the candy slice and roll a full food can over it. Use a bit of frosting to attach it below and to the right of the eye.

Flat-ice the tail with orange frosting.

GINGERBREAD HOUSE

The perfect holiday birthday treat, you can either decorate it ahead of time or simply flat-ice it and treat it like a traditional gingerbread house and leave it up to the party-goers to add the candy. I've included the directions to match my design, but it's always more fun to use your favorite candies to create your own masterpiece.

You Will Need:

- 1 recipe Pound Cake (page 41) or Cake Mix Fix (page 43)*
- cutting board
- serrated knife
- 1 recipe Basic Buttercream (the lemon variation goes great with spice cake—page 46)
- brown food coloring (or 2 tablespoons cocoa powder + red food coloring)
- piping bag
- coupler and ring
- basketweave tip (#47)
- small round tip (#3)
- ¼ cup M&M's
- 2 tablespoons M&M's Minis
- 8 yellow Starburst Minis
- red and green gumdrops
- 2 candy canes
- 3 spearmint leaves
- cutting board
- sharp knife

*__Note:__ For a gingerbread-like spice cake taste, leave out the vanilla and add 1½ teaspoon cinnamon + 1½ teaspoon ginger + ⅛ teaspoon cloves + ⅛ teaspoon nutmeg.

How to Decorate Gingerbread House

Scoop 1 cup white frosting into a piping bag with a coupler and your small round tip (#3). Set it aside.

Color the remaining frosting reddish brown using cocoa powder and red food coloring, or brown food coloring if your cake's flavor is not compatible with chocolate. Cover it and set it aside.

De-pan the cake and cut it according to the diagram found at the back of this book. If you wish to torte and fill the cake, torte and fill the individual pieces after cutting out the shapes to reduce leakage.

Place the two triangle pieces at the top of the large rectangular piece to form a house shape. Do not attach the chimney.

Crumb-coat and flat-ice the house with the reddish-brown frosting.

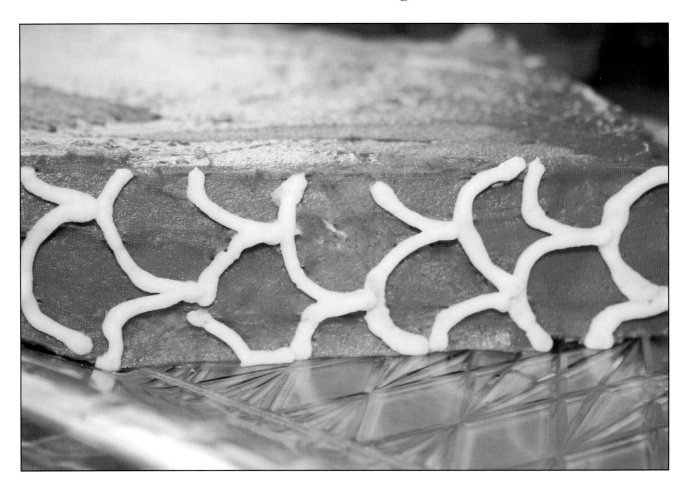

Use the bag of white frosting to pipe swooping tiles on the side of the roof of the house.

Flat-ice the two sides of the chimney with the reddish-brown frosting, then carefully nestle it into the roof. Flat-ice the top of the chimney with more reddish-brown frosting. Use your piping bag of white frosting to pipe bricks onto the chimney.

Remove the small round tip, and replace it with the basketweave tip (#47).

With the serrated edge of the tip facing the cake, frost straight lines along the outside edges of the house.

Pipe swooping lines along the outside edges of the roof.

Fill in the gaps by piping small lines, and use a finger to blend frosting together.

Place an M&M on each swoop, alternating colors in a pattern.

Frost the outlines of a door and two windows.

Place four yellow Starburst Minis inside each window frame, and frost lines between them as window panes.

Place a brown M&M as the doorknob.

Place a line of M&M's Minis on the frosted door frame.

Remove the basketweave tip from your piping bag and replace it with the small round tip. Frost icicles under each roof swoop (where your M&M's are) by holding the bag at a 45° angle. Squeeze gently and pull down, releasing pressure as you move. Repeat icicle technique on the top edge of the chimney.

Break the rounded pieces off of both candy canes. Place the remaining straight candy cane pieces to either side of the door.

Place a red gumdrop at the top of each candy cane piece.

Slice a green gumdrop in half lengthwise. Place one half on the outside side of each candy cane.

Slice three spearmint leaves in half front-to-back. Arrange them in a circle above the windows.

Place one red M&M's Mini on each leaf.

HOT AIR BALLOON

You will feel like you're flying away with this beautiful balloon cake.

You Will Need:

- 1 recipe Pound Cake (page 41) or Cake Mix Fix (page 43), baked in a small metal mixing bowl + 1 cupcake (baked without a wrapper)*
- large serrated knife
- cutting board
- 1 recipe Basic Buttercream (page 46)
- red, yellow, and blue food coloring

- 7 small bowls (or clean and reuse a single bowl)
- 1 teaspoon cocoa powder
- 1 piping bag
- 1 coupler and ring
- medium star tip (#21)
- basketweave tip (#47)
- black licorice shoelace candy

*Metal mixing bowls come in different sizes. Because the cake expands while baking, you don't want to fill it more than two-thirds full. If you have leftover batter, bake it in the bottom of a 9 x 13-inch pan. Tint 1 cup of your Basic Buttercream sky blue, and flat-ice the 9 x 13 cake with it. Assemble your hot air balloon on top of this cake.

How to Assemble Hot Air Balloon Cake

De-pan the cake and cupcake.

Level the tops of the cake and cupcake (the part that was not in the pan while baking).

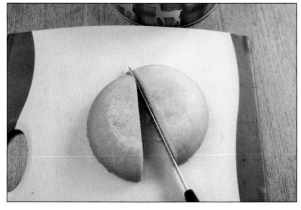

Place the cake upside down on the cutting board. Use your serrated knife to slice the cake in half vertically.

Place one half of the cake on the cake board, so the just-cut edge of the cake is facing down, and the top of the cake (when it was baking in the pan) is facing you. Place the other half of the cake right beside it so the top of this half is touching the top of the other half, and the just-cut side is facing down

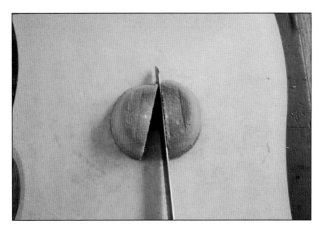

Sit the cupcake on your cutting board and slice it in half, just like you did the cake.

Place one half of the cupcake cut-side down, beside the cake, so the top of the cupcake (when it was baking) is touching the base of the cake.

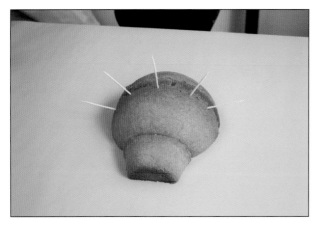

Use toothpicks to divide the widest part of the cake into six sections.

Scoop ½ cup Basic Buttercream into a small bowl and tint it dark pink or red. Place the dark pink/red frosting into a piping bag with your large star tip (#21). Pipe a line of stars along where the left-most toothpick is marking, then remove the toothpick. Pipe red stars to fill in the remaining area of that section. Empty the piping bag, wash and dry it and the tip thoroughly.

Scoop ½ cup Basic Buttercream into a small bowl. Tint it orange with yellow and red food coloring. Place the orange frosting and the large star tip into the piping bag and pipe a line of stars along the mark of the next toothpick. Remove the toothpick.

Pipe orange stars to fill in the section between the orange line and the red area.

Empty any remaining frosting from the bag, and thoroughly clean and dry it and tip.

Scoop ½ cup Basic Buttercream into a small bowl. Tint it yellow and place it in piping bag with medium star tip. Pipe a line of stars along the mark of the next toothpick. Fill in section with yellow stars.

Empty the remaining frosting and thoroughly clean and dry the bag and tip.

Continue this for the next three colors (green, blue, and purple), until the entire balloon is covered in stars.

Scoop ½ cup Basic Buttercream into a small bowl. Stir in ½ teaspoon cocoa powder and yellow food coloring to tint it tan. Place the tan frosting in a piping bag with a coupler and the basketweave tip (#47).

Place the second half of the cupcake on the serving plate, about two inches below the balloon cake.

Use the serrated side of the basketweave tip to pipe serrated lines across the bottom of the cupcake.

Pipe basketweave over the sides of the cupcake (see page 28 for instructions).

Remove the basketweave tip and place the large star tip on the piping bag. Pipe a line across the top edge of the cupcake.

Cut four 2-inch lengths of black licorice shoelace candy and gently push them into the bottom of the balloon cake and the top of the basket cake, joining the two together.

DELICIOUS DRAGON #1

These fabulous creatures are among my favorite designs. In fact, I love them so much, I've included two different variations: one with piped scales and candy accents, and another no-piping-required dragon using flat-icing and candy.

Delicious Dragon #1

This cute little guy takes some time and a steady hand, but I think you'll find the effort is worth it.

You Will Need:

- 1 recipe Pound Cake (page 41), or Cake Mix Fix (page 43), baked as two 8-inch rounds
- serrated knife
- cutting board
- 1 recipe Basic Buttercream (page 46)
- blue and green gel food coloring
- piping bag
- sharp knife
- 2 large candy eyeballs
- 10–12 orange Starburst Minis
- 2 brown M&M's Minis
- 8 orange M&M's (have more just in case they shatter when cutting)
- 2 orange jelly beans
- cupcake-filling tip (#230)
- 1 tube red Decorator's Icing
- small round tip (#3) compatible with Decorator's Icing tube

How to Assemble and Decorate Delicious Dragon #1

Sit both cakes on a cutting board right-side up (the way they cooked in the pan)—don't worry if your cake has puffed up; it simply makes your dragon a bit chubbier.

Using your serrated knife, cut out the dragon according to the template provided at the back of this book—these directions are for a dragon with his head on the right, tail on the left. If you want your dragon to face the other direction, flip the cake upside down before cutting (but still use the pieces right-side up).

Tint your Basic Buttercream blue, and use some to flat-ice the bottom of one of the dragon body cake halves.

Stick the bottoms of the two dragon body pieces together, and center them on your serving plate, sitting them cut-side down. Assemble the rest of the pieces of dragon, as shown above, using frosting as glue to hold the pieces together.

Use a sharp knife to cut 5 of the Starburst Minis in half. Cut 3 into thirds, and cut the corners off of the remaining two. This will give you three sizes of spikes for the dragon's back.

Cut your orange M&M's in half—these will be the dragon's claws (they shatter easily, so I suggest having a few spares on hand).

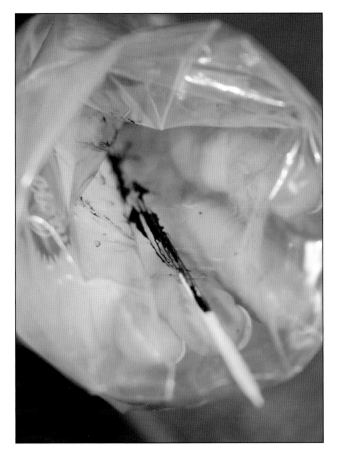

Place the cupcake-filling tip (#230) in a piping bag. Dip a toothpick in your green gel food coloring, and use it to stripe three lines inside your piping bag—this streaks color onto your scales as you pipe, giving them more character. If you don't have gel colors on hand, simply skip this step and pipe plain blue scales—liquid food coloring doesn't really work for this trick.

Place about ⅔ cup of blue frosting into the bag—do not overfill. Because of how long it takes to pipe the scales, you'll want to refill a few times with fresh frosting, since the heat of your hands can cause the frosting to break. If you notice your frosting getting soft at any point, take a break and stick your piping bag into the fridge for five minutes to cool it down. If your frosting does end up breaking, squeeze it out of the bag and replace it with fresh frosting. Remember, every time you refill your bag, you'll want to re-line it with green gel food coloring.

Piping scales uses a lot of frosting, so I actually don't recommend crumb-coating your dragon before piping—just be careful not to touch the piping tip to the cut edges of cake, or you'll pick up crumbs. If you do end up with crumbs in your scales, simply pick them out carefully with a toothpick or skewer.

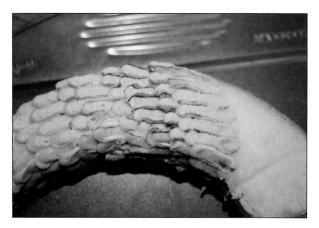

Starting at the tip of the tail, pipe scales in a bricklay pattern, as explained on page 31. Continue working your way from the back of the dragon forward, covering both sides and the top of the dragon.

While the frosting is still wet, gently press some of your Starburst Mini spikes into the dragon's back in a line, starting with the smallest, and getting larger as your reach his body.

Continue piping scales over the dragon's body and legs. Once you have finished the dragon's legs and belly, carefully slide four half-M&M's, cut-side down, into the front of the back legs, and three halves in the front of each of the front legs. Continue piping scales over the neck and head, and continue the line of Starburst Mini spikes, placing increasingly smaller spikes from the body to the head.

Place one orange jelly bean on either side of the spike on the dragon's head.

Place the two candy eyeballs on the front of the dragon's head. Place the two brown M&M's Minis on the front of the dragon's nose.

Attach the small round compatible tip to the tube of Decorator's Icing and pipe a smile under the dragon's nose.

DELICIOUS DRAGON #2

This variation requires no piping skills, simply flat-icing and candy. I have given directions to recreate the dragon in the photo exactly, but feel free to mix and match the colors of your choice—however, I do recommend using at three colors of M&M's for the scales, both because it looks better, and because it cuts down on the number of bags of candy you have to buy.

You Will Need:
- 1 recipe Pound Cake (page 41), or Cake Mix Fix (page 43), baked as two 8-inch rounds
- 1 frosting recipe
- 2 tablespoons cocoa powder, or food coloring to match one color of the scales
- serrated knife
- cutting board
- 2 cups each, red, brown, and orange M&M's
- ¼ cup each, red, brown, and orange M&M's Minis
- 2 large candy eyeballs
- 15 yellow Starburst Minis
- 8 yellow M&M's (have more just in case they shatter when cutting)
- 2 yellow jelly beans
- sharp knife
- Life Saver Fire, optional (page 38)

How to Decorate Delicious Dragon #2
Use the cocoa powder or food coloring to tint your frosting the same color as one of your scales (I used Fudgy Chocolate Frosting for my dragon—page 47).

Cut your cakes and assemble them according to the directions in Delicious Dragon #1, substituting your frosting for the blue frosting in those instructions.

Starting at the tip of the tail, flat-ice a small portion of the dragon (not too much; you don't want the frosting to harden or the M&M's won't stick to it), and lay out M&M's Minis in a bricklay pattern, alternating the colors randomly. After 2–3 rows of M&M's Minis, start laying down full-size M&M's onto the dragon.

Continue flat-icing in patches, and laying down M&M's— use your M&M's Minis to fill in any small gaps—until you have covered the entire dragon.

Cut your yellow M&M's in half and press four halves, cut-side down, into the front of each back leg, and three M&M halves into the front of each front leg, as claws.

Cut your Starburst Minis according to the directions in Delicious Dragon #1. Dab a small amount of frosting onto the bottom of the one of the smallest Starburst Mini spikes, and gently sit it on top of the tail. Continue adding Starburst Mini spikes in a line up the dragon's back, going from the smallest on its tail to the largest on its back, back to small ones on its head.

Carefully push one yellow jelly bean on either side of the last spike on the dragon's head (you may need to remove an M&M scale or two for this to fit).

Dab a bit of frosting onto the back of each of the two eyeballs, and gently press them onto the front of the dragon's head.

If you want, carefully press a piece of Life Saver Fire into the front of the dragon's snout, just before serving (if you do it too early, the fire will absorb moisture from the cake and melt into an oozing mess).

CONVERSION CHARTS

METRIC AND IMPERIAL CONVERSIONS

(These conversions are rounded for convenience)

Ingredient	Cups/Tablespoons/Teaspoons	Ounces	Grams/Milliliters
Butter	1 cup=16 tablespoons= 2 sticks	8 ounces	230 grams
Cream cheese	1 tablespoon	0.5 ounce	14.5 grams
Cheese, shredded	1 cup	4 ounces	110 grams
Cornstarch	1 tablespoon	0.3 ounce	8 grams
Flour, all-purpose	1 cup/1 tablespoon	4.5 ounces/0.3 ounce	125 grams/8 grams
Flour, whole wheat	1 cup	4 ounces	120 grams
Fruit, dried	1 cup	4 ounces	120 grams
Fruits or veggies, chopped	1 cup	5 to 7 ounces	145 to 200 grams
Fruits or veggies, puréed	1 cup	8.5 ounces	245 grams
Honey, maple syrup, or corn syrup	1 tablespoon	.75 ounce	20 grams
Liquids: cream, milk, water, or juice	1 cup	8 fluid ounces	240 milliliters
Oats	1 cup	5.5 ounces	150 grams
Salt	1 teaspoon	0.2 ounces	6 grams
Spices: cinnamon, cloves, ginger, or nutmeg (ground)	1 teaspoon	0.2 ounce	5 milliliters
Sugar, brown, firmly packed	1 cup	7 ounces	200 grams
Sugar, white	1 cup/1 tablespoon	7 ounces/0.5 ounce	200 grams/12.5 grams
Vanilla extract	1 teaspoon	0.2 ounce	4 grams

OVEN TEMPERATURES

Fahrenheit	Celcius	Gas Mark
225°	110°	¼
250°	120°	½
275°	140°	1
300°	150°	2
325°	160°	3
350°	180°	4
375°	190°	5
400°	200°	6
425°	220°	7
450°	230°	8

INDEX

TEMPLATES AND DIAGRAMS

Simple Starburst Cake

Stunning Snowflakes

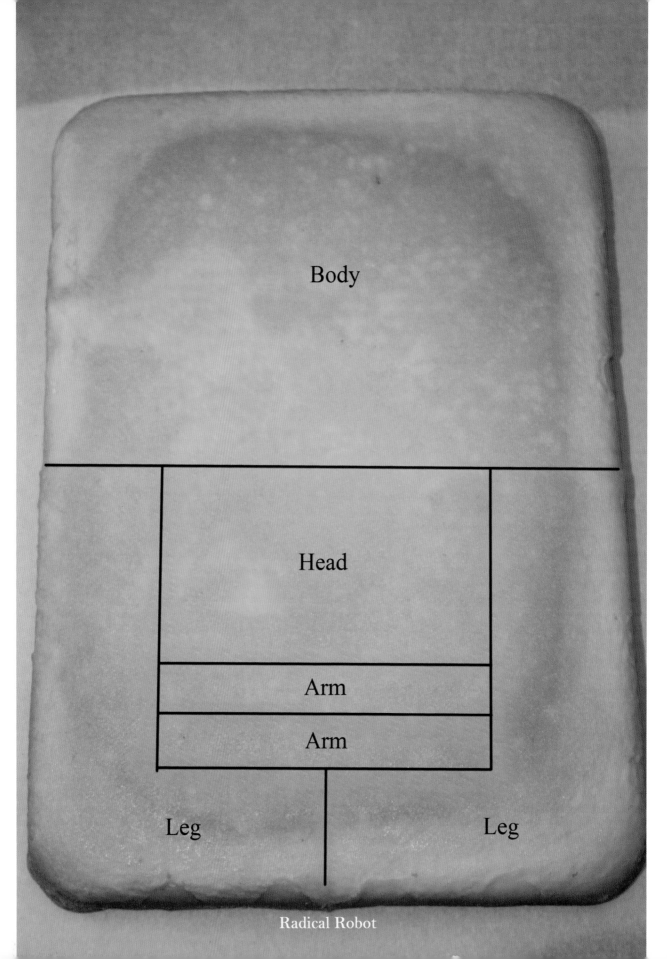

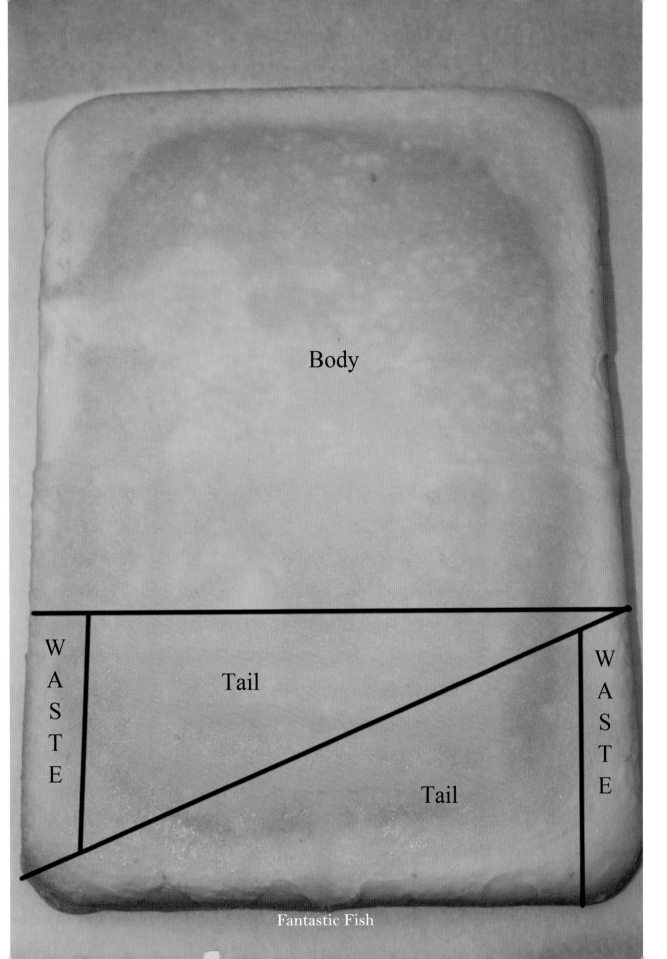

Fabulous Flamingo

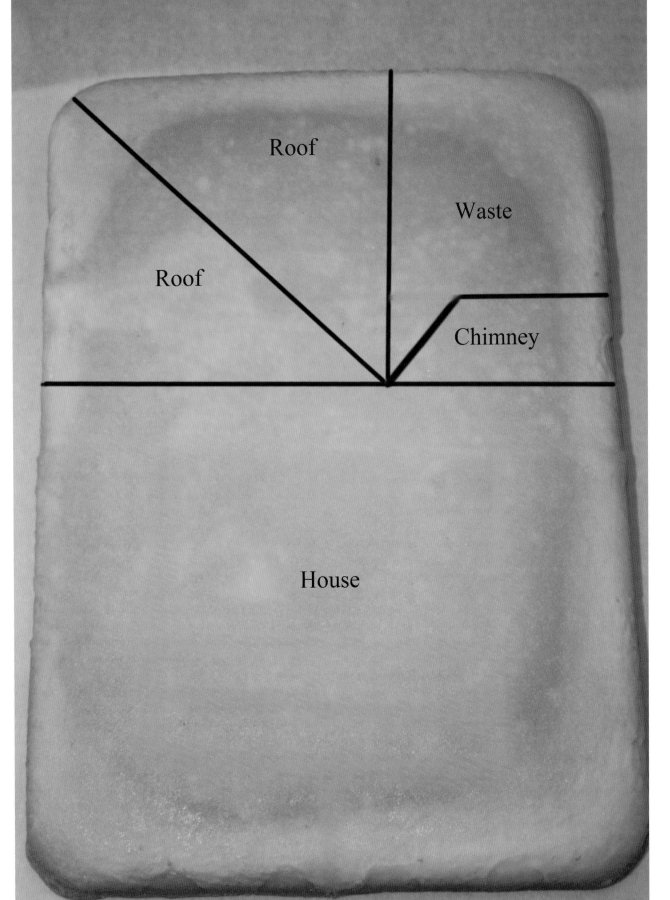
Gingerbread House

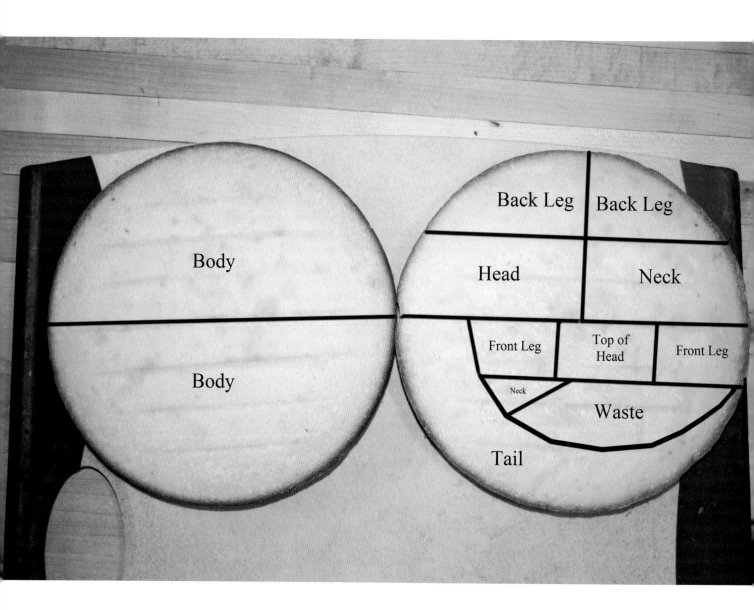

Delicious Dragons